Skyscrapers Coloring Book

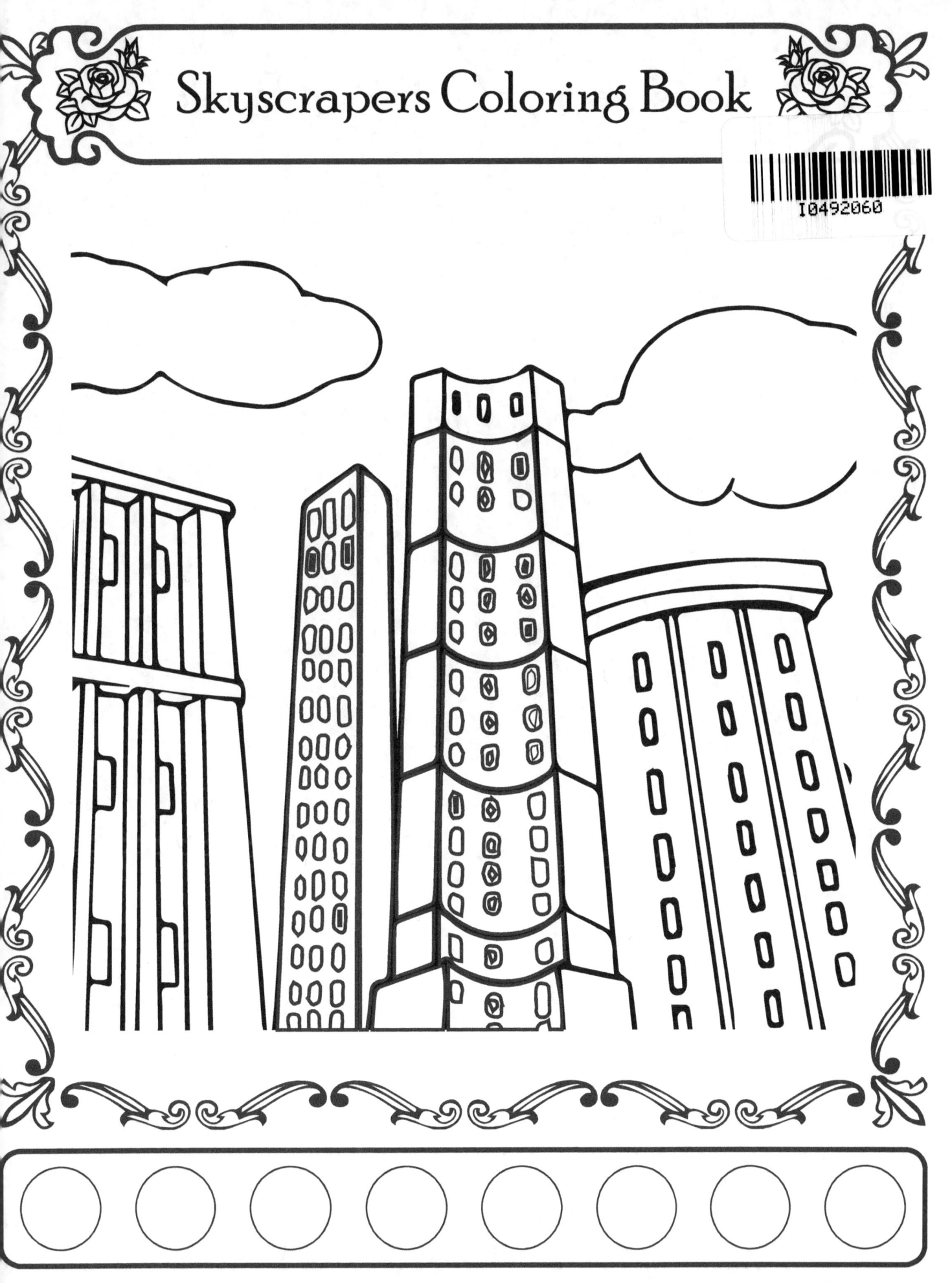

Skyscrapers Coloring Book

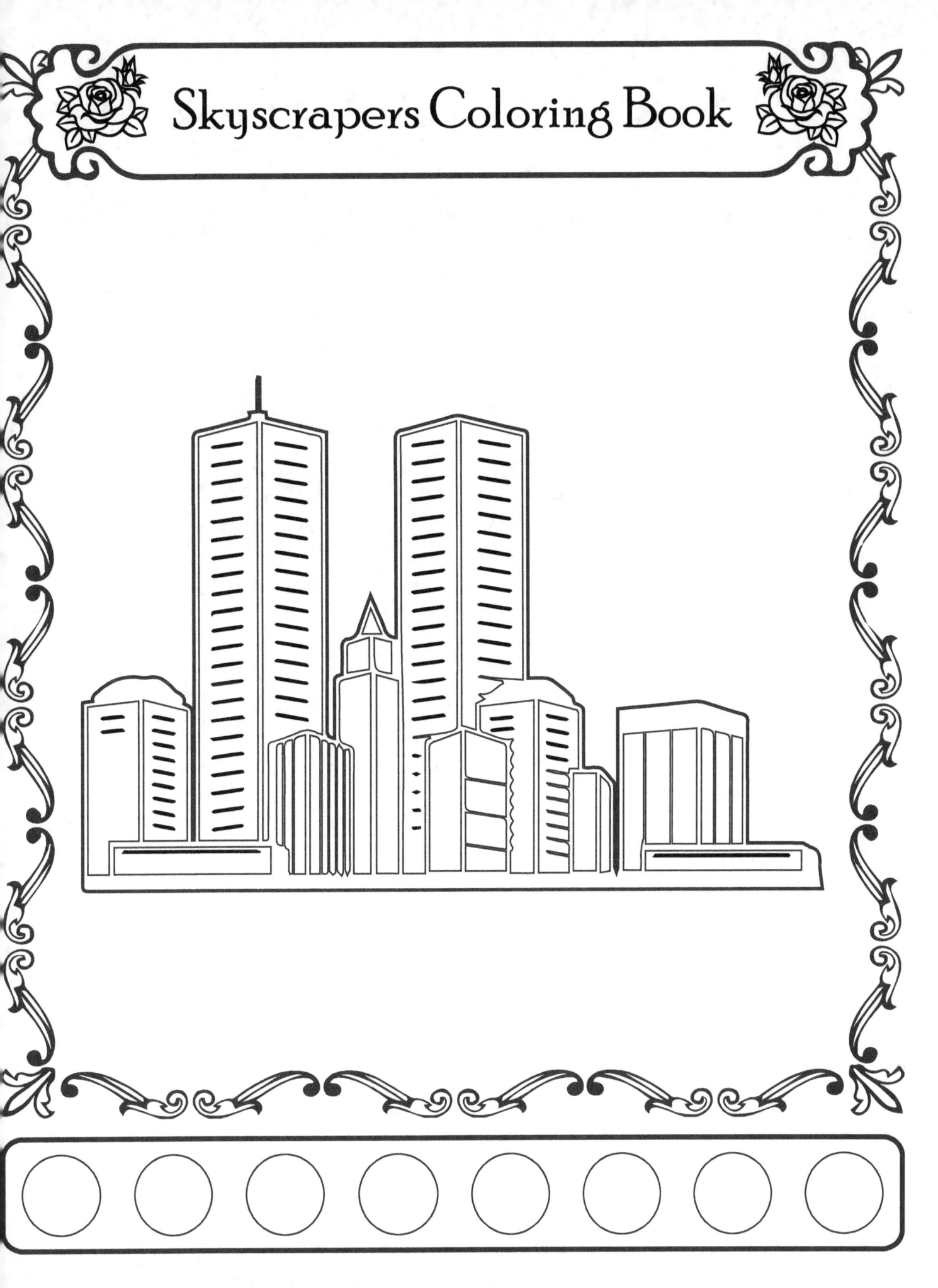

Skyscrapers Coloring Book

Skyscrapers Coloring Book

Skyscrapers Coloring Book

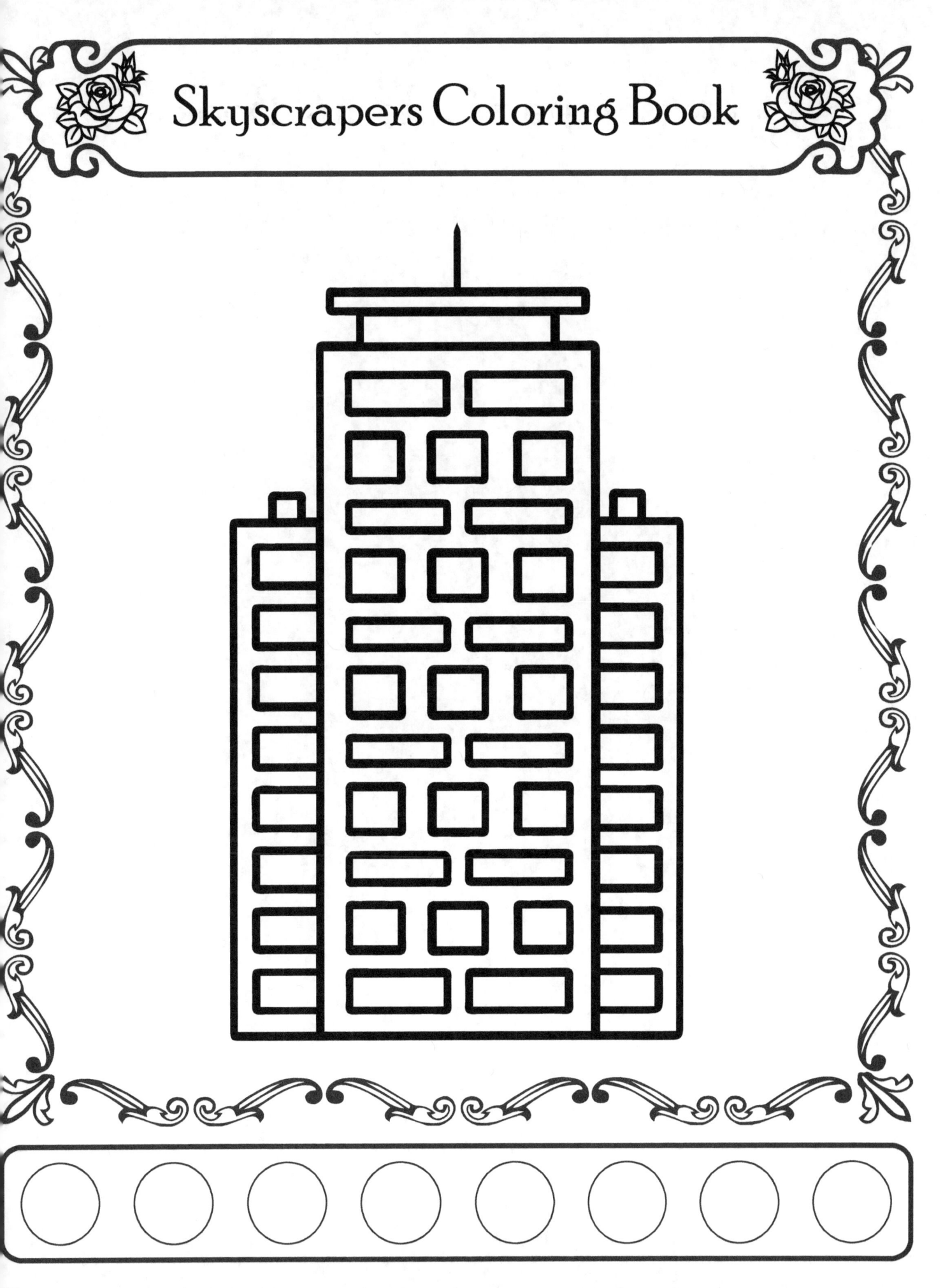

Skyscrapers Coloring Book

Skyscrapers Coloring Book

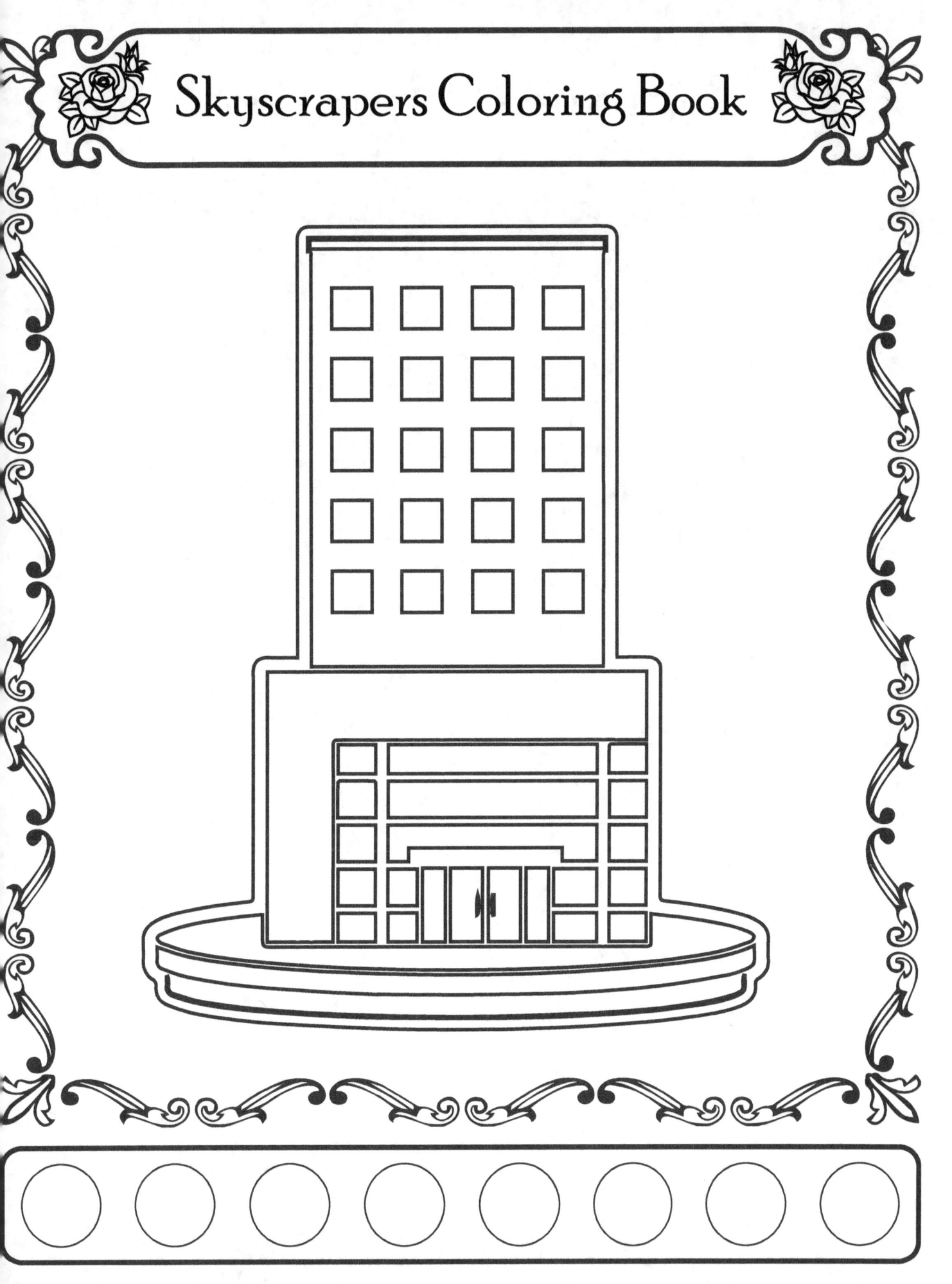

Skyscrapers Coloring Book

Skyscrapers Coloring Book

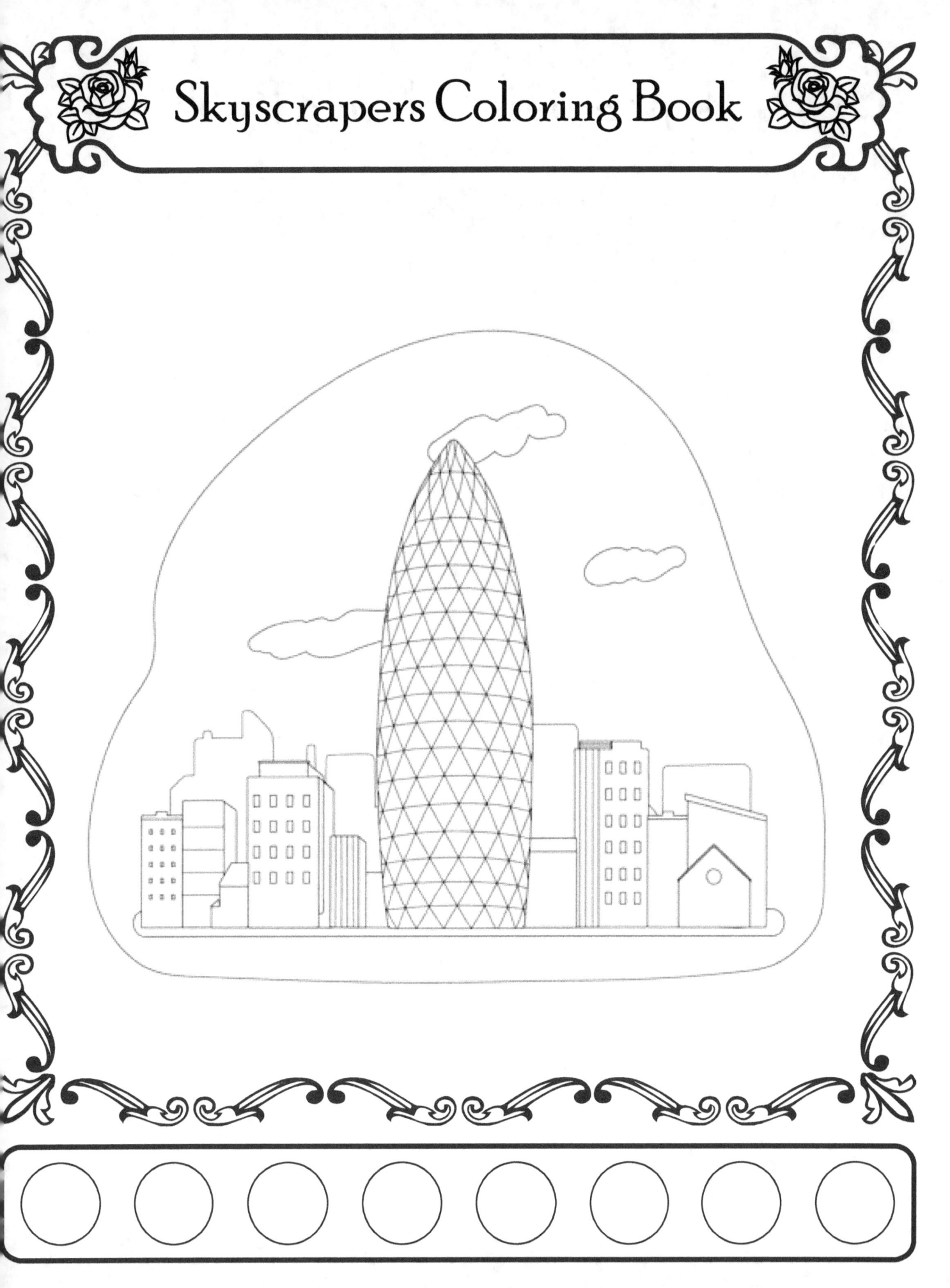

Skyscrapers Coloring Book

Skyscrapers Coloring Book

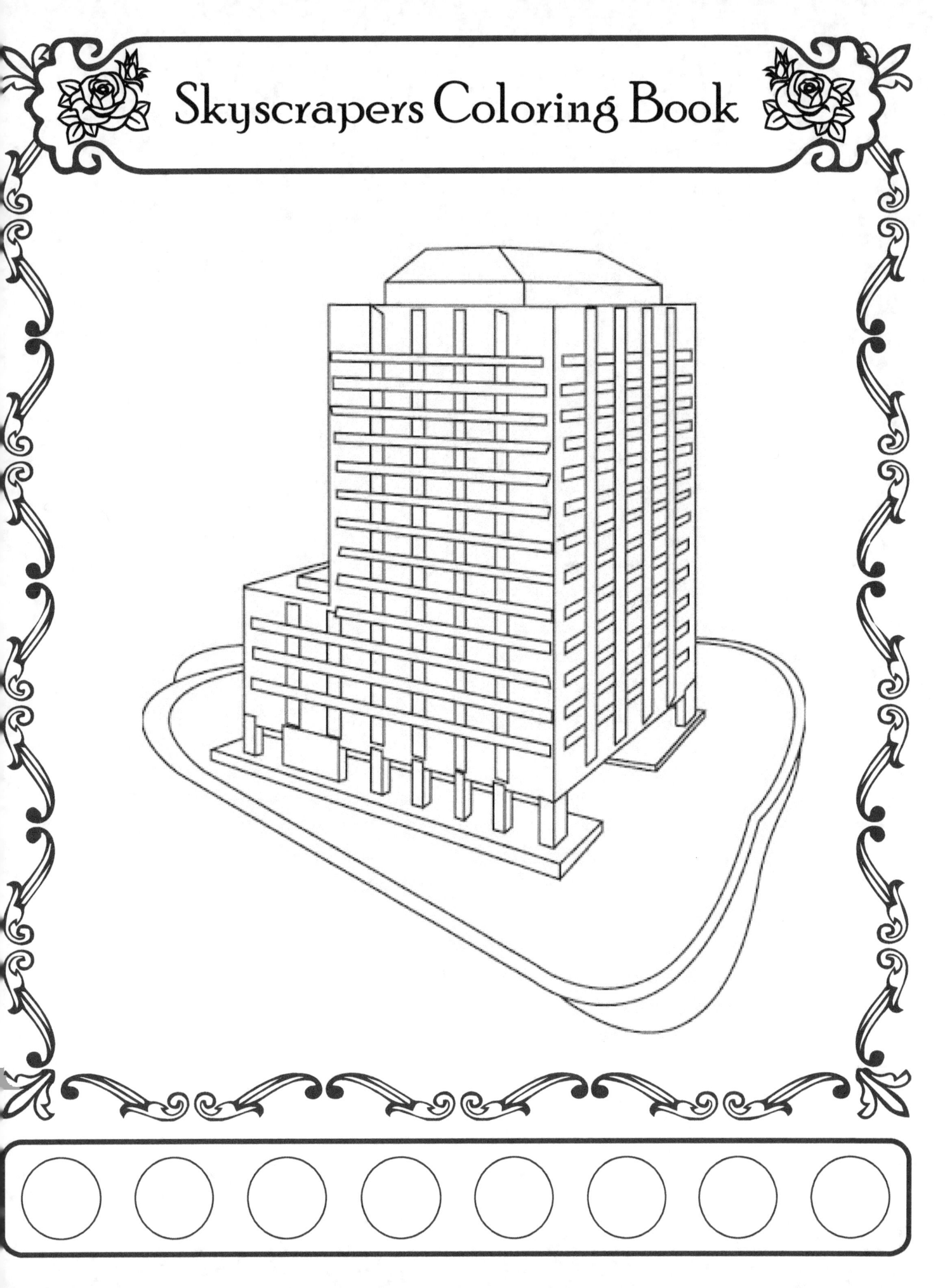

Skyscrapers Coloring Book

Skyscrapers Coloring Book

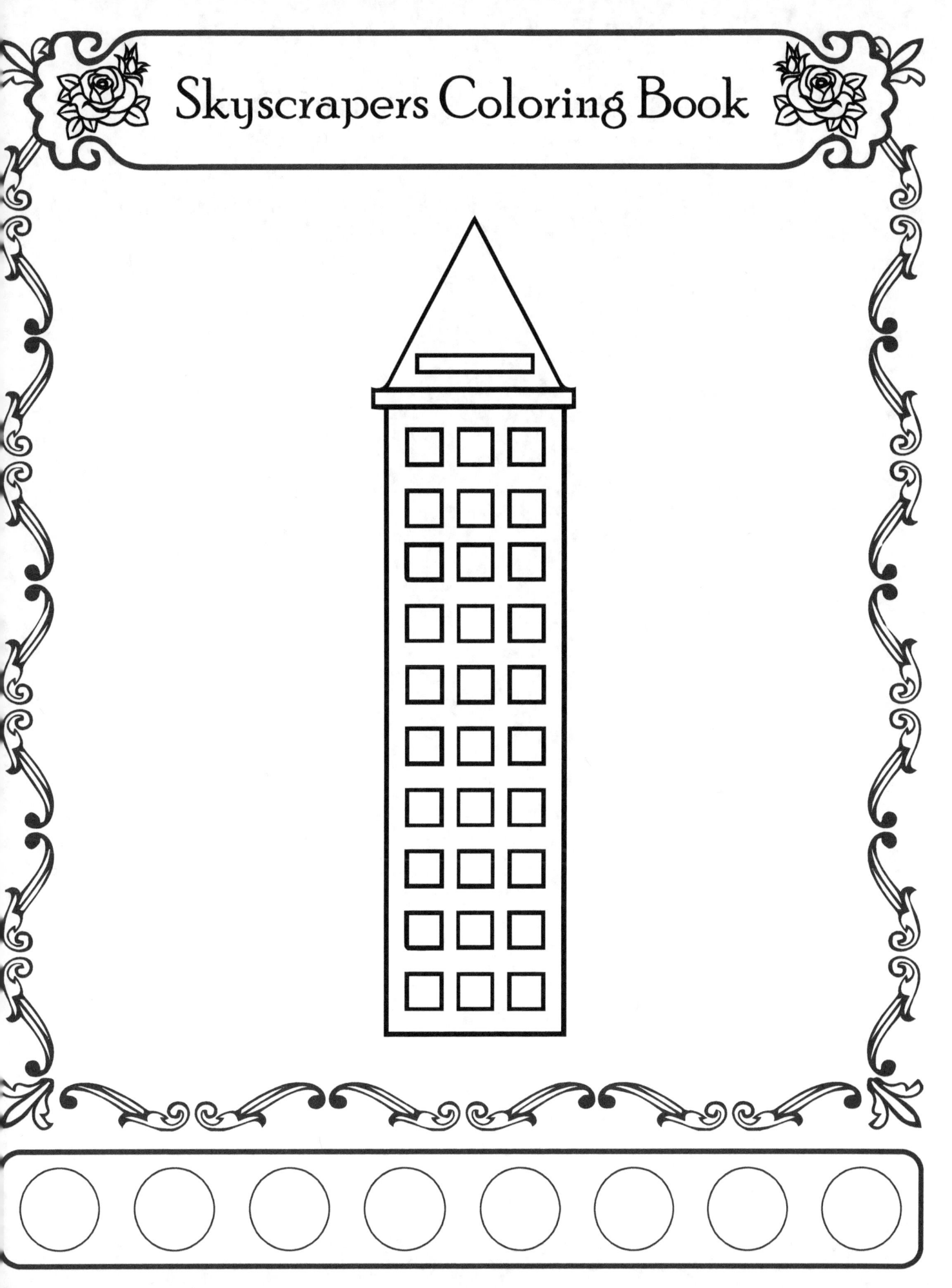

Skyscrapers Coloring Book

Skyscrapers Coloring Book

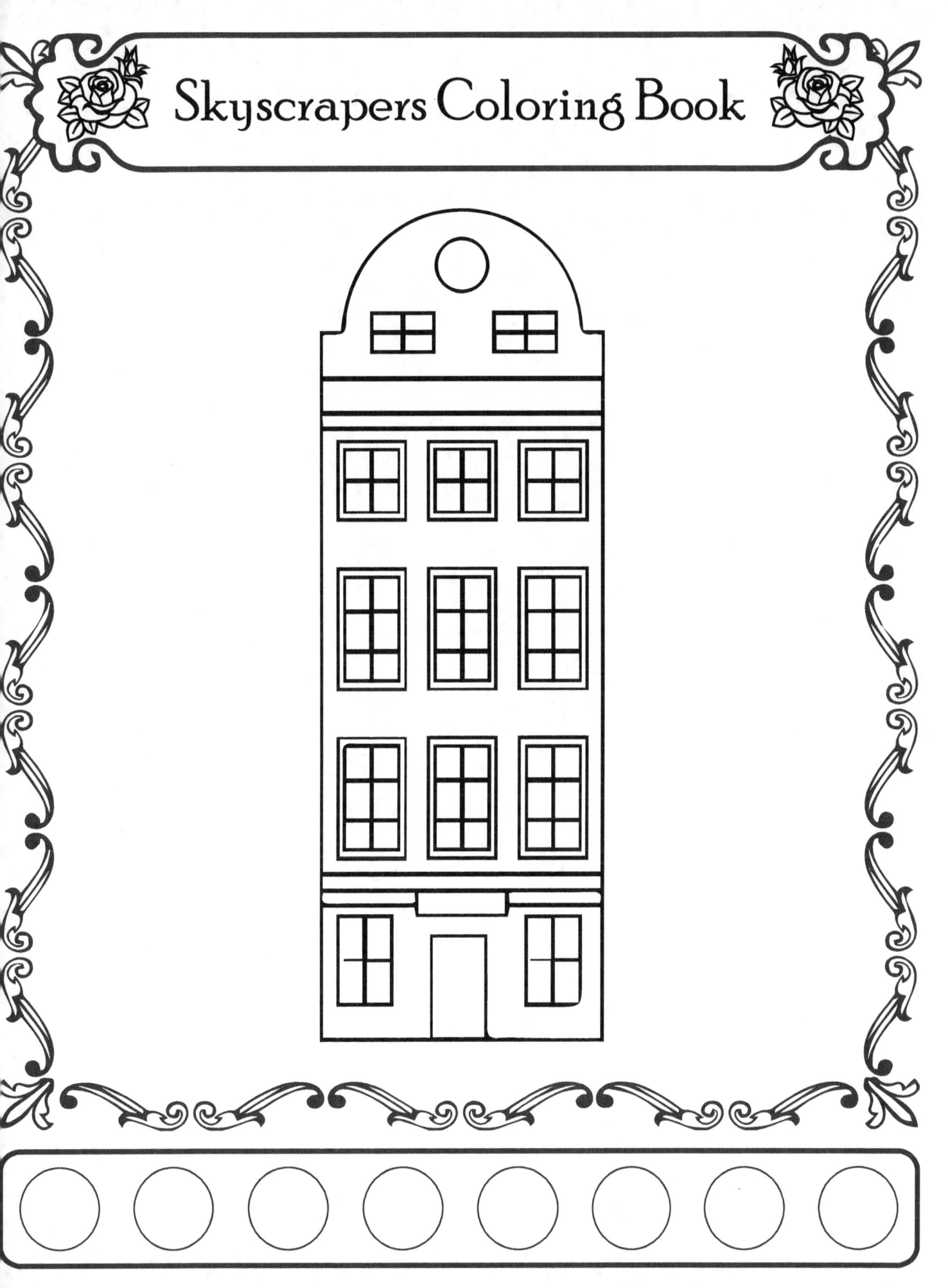

Skyscrapers Coloring Book

Skyscrapers Coloring Book

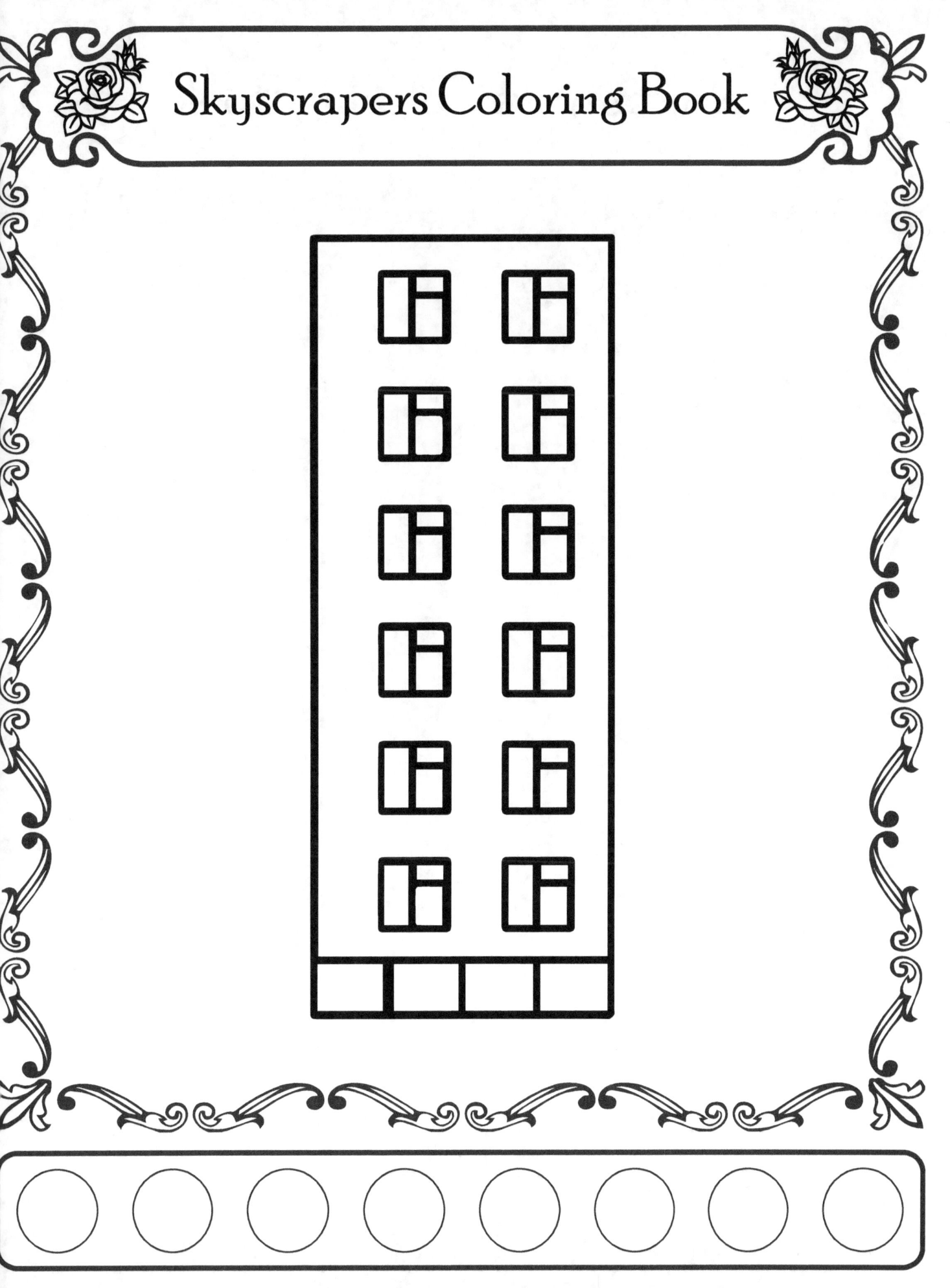

Skyscrapers Coloring Book

Skyscrapers Coloring Book

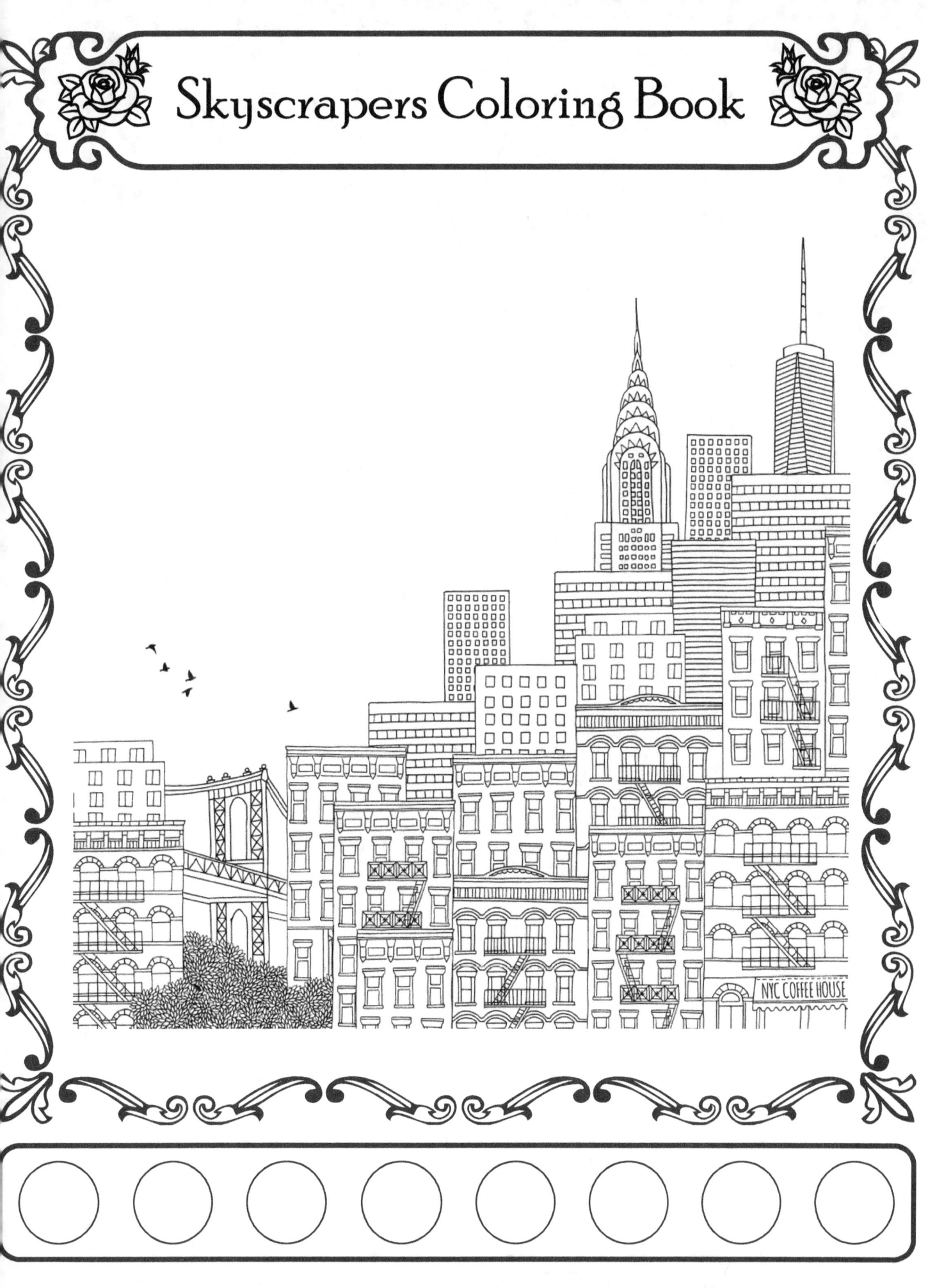

Skyscrapers Coloring Book

Skyscrapers Coloring Book

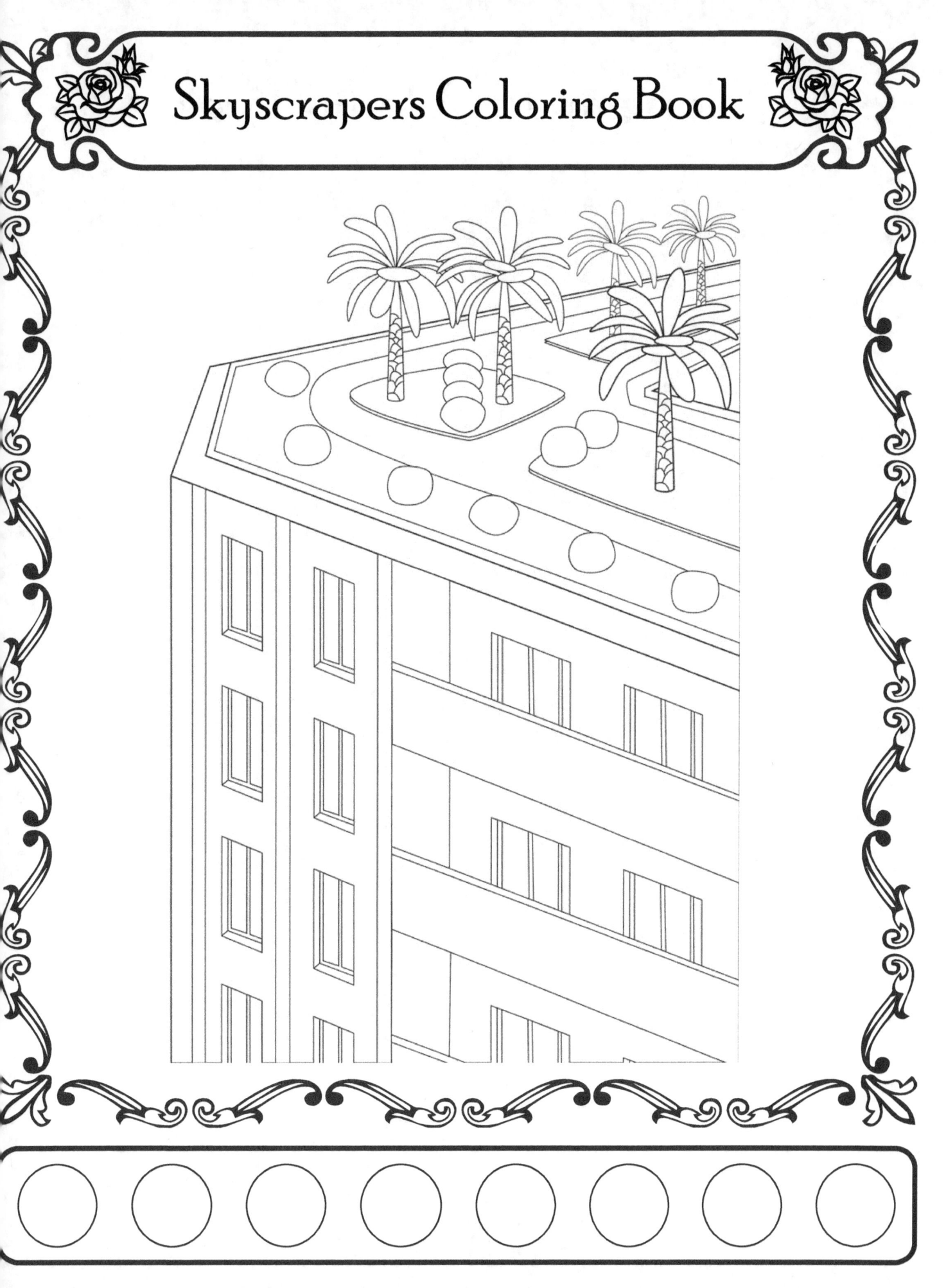

Skyscrapers Coloring Book

Skyscrapers Coloring Book

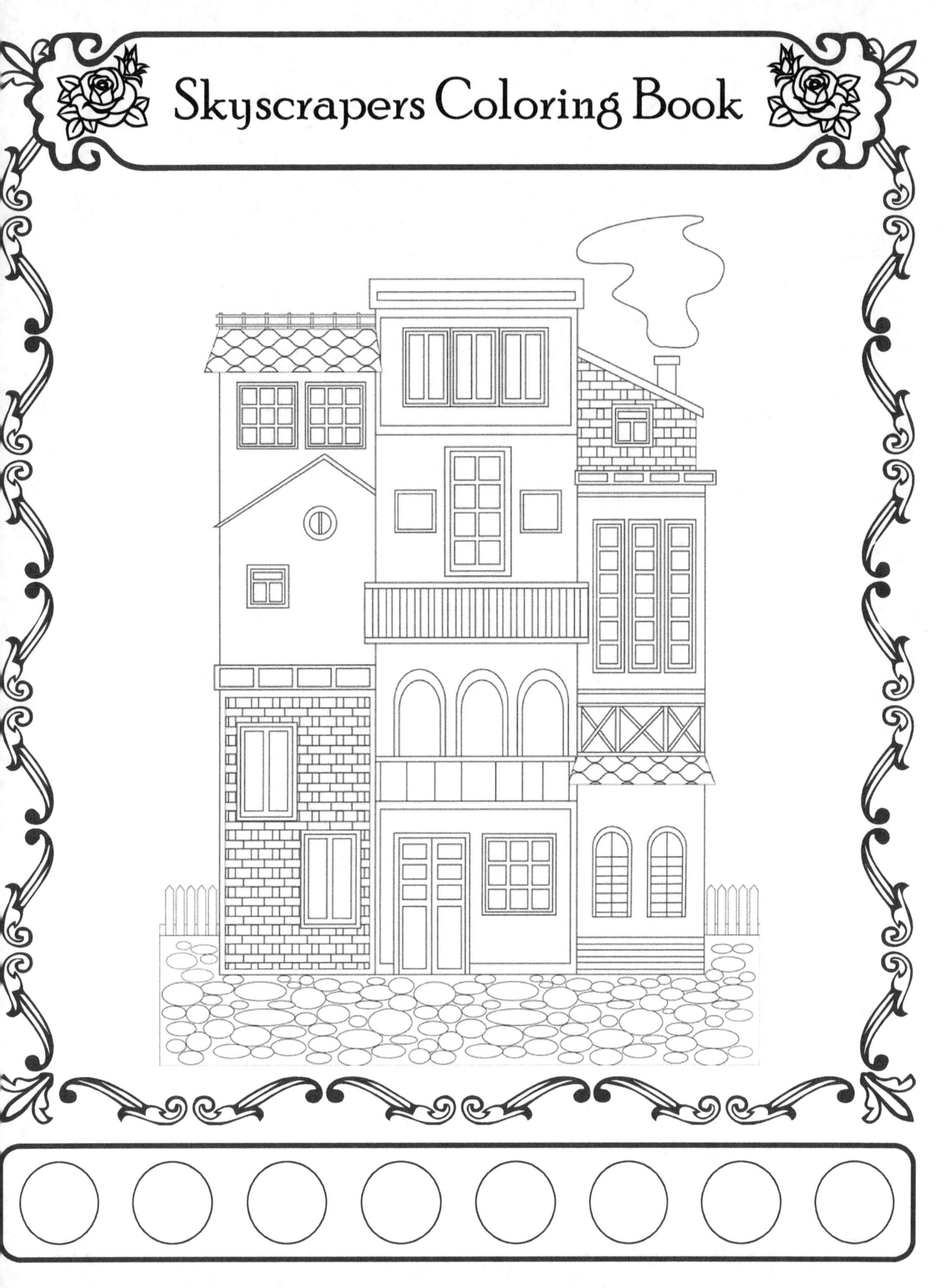

Skyscrapers Coloring Book

Skyscrapers Coloring Book

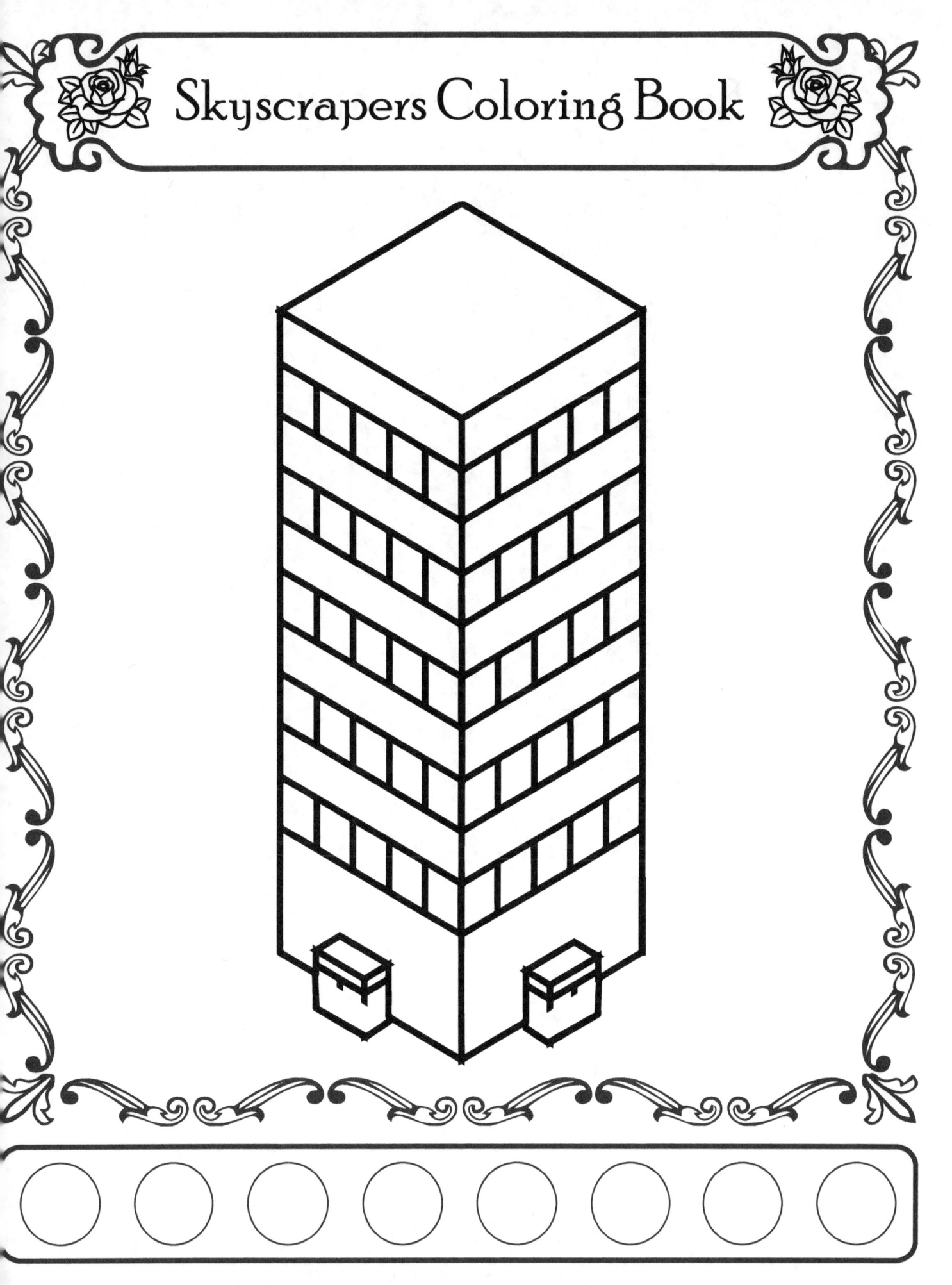

Skyscrapers Coloring Book

Skyscrapers Coloring Book

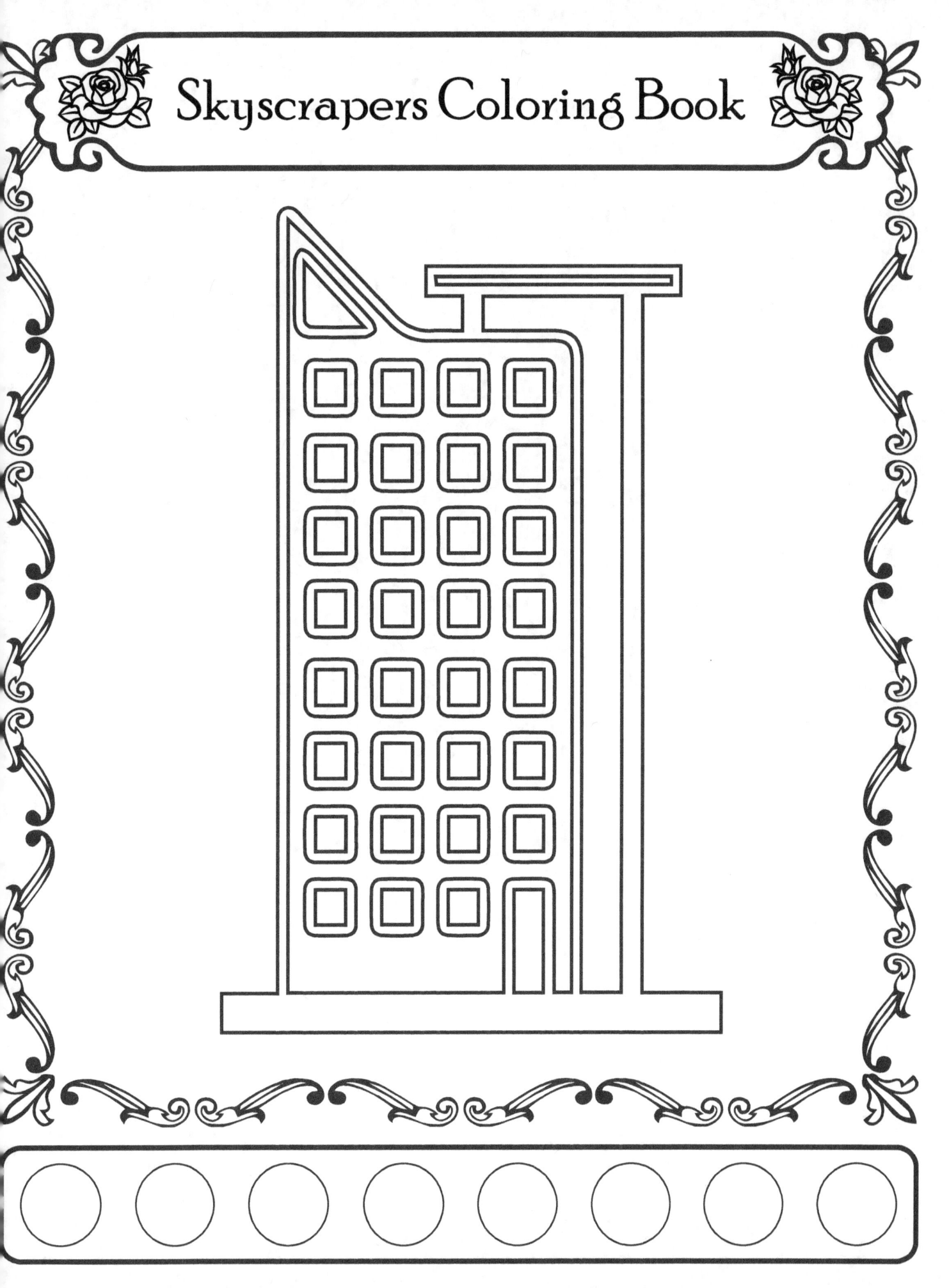

Skyscrapers Coloring Book

Skyscrapers Coloring Book

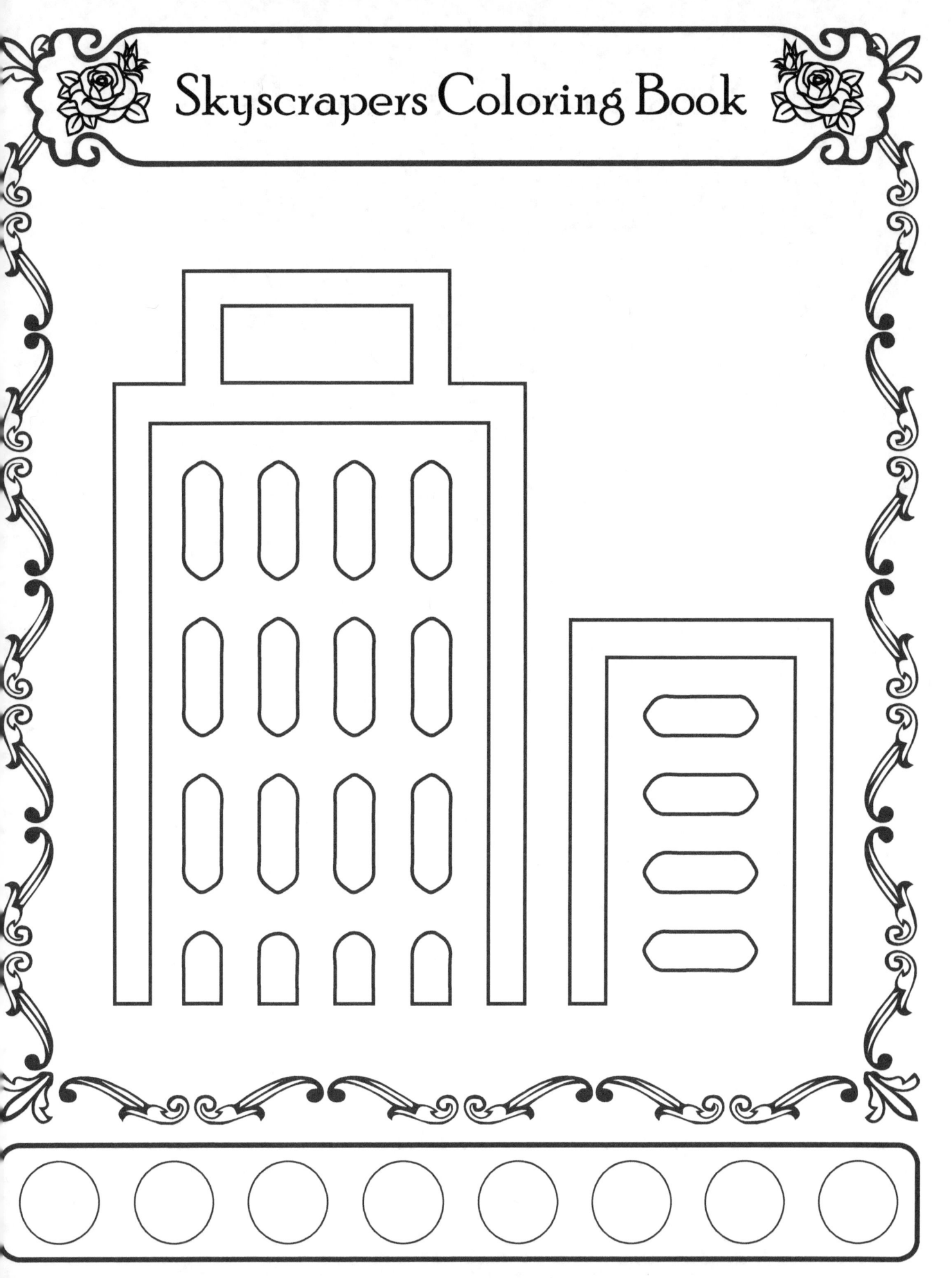

Skyscrapers Coloring Book

Skyscrapers Coloring Book

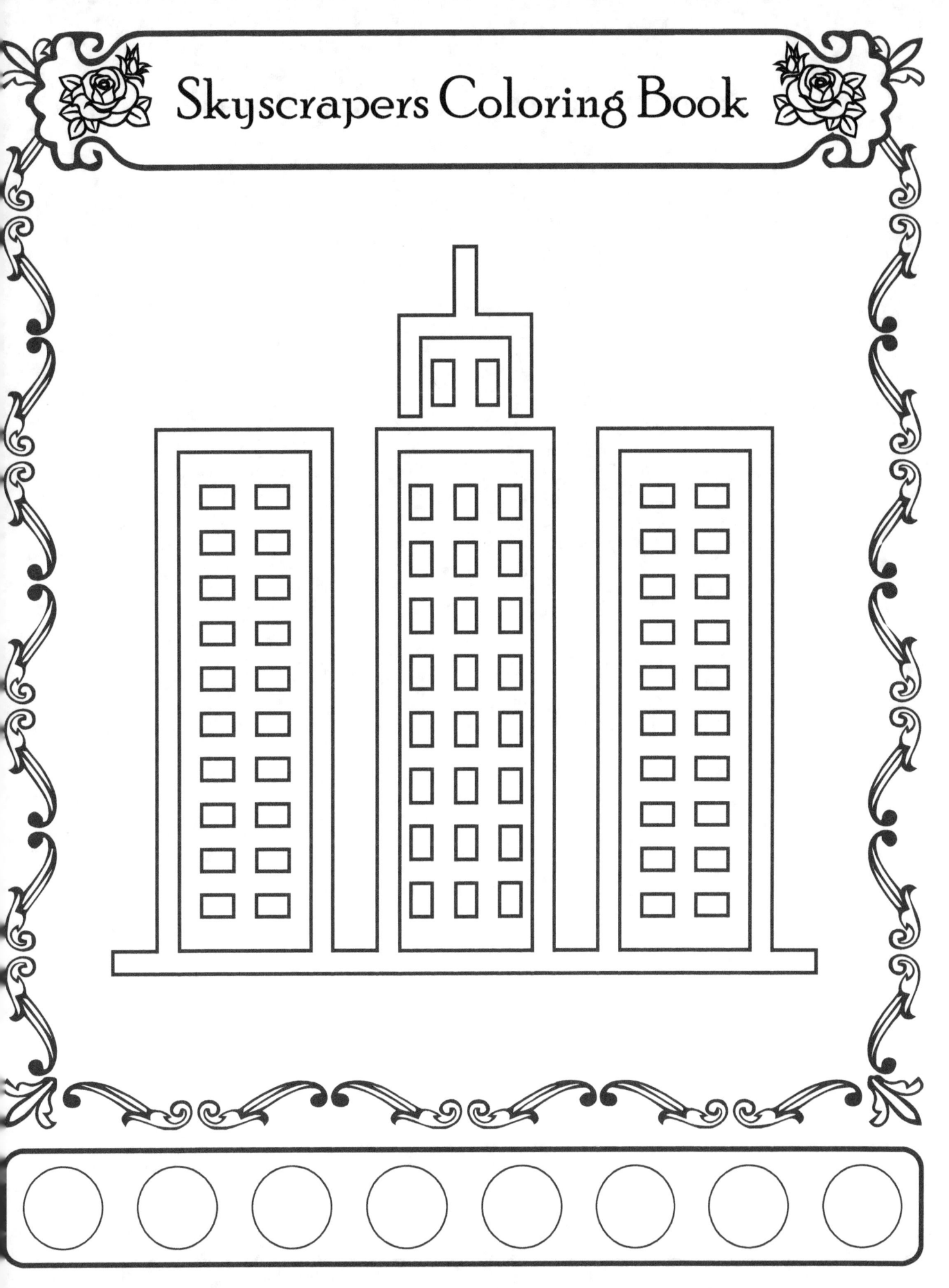

Skyscrapers Coloring Book

Skyscrapers Coloring Book

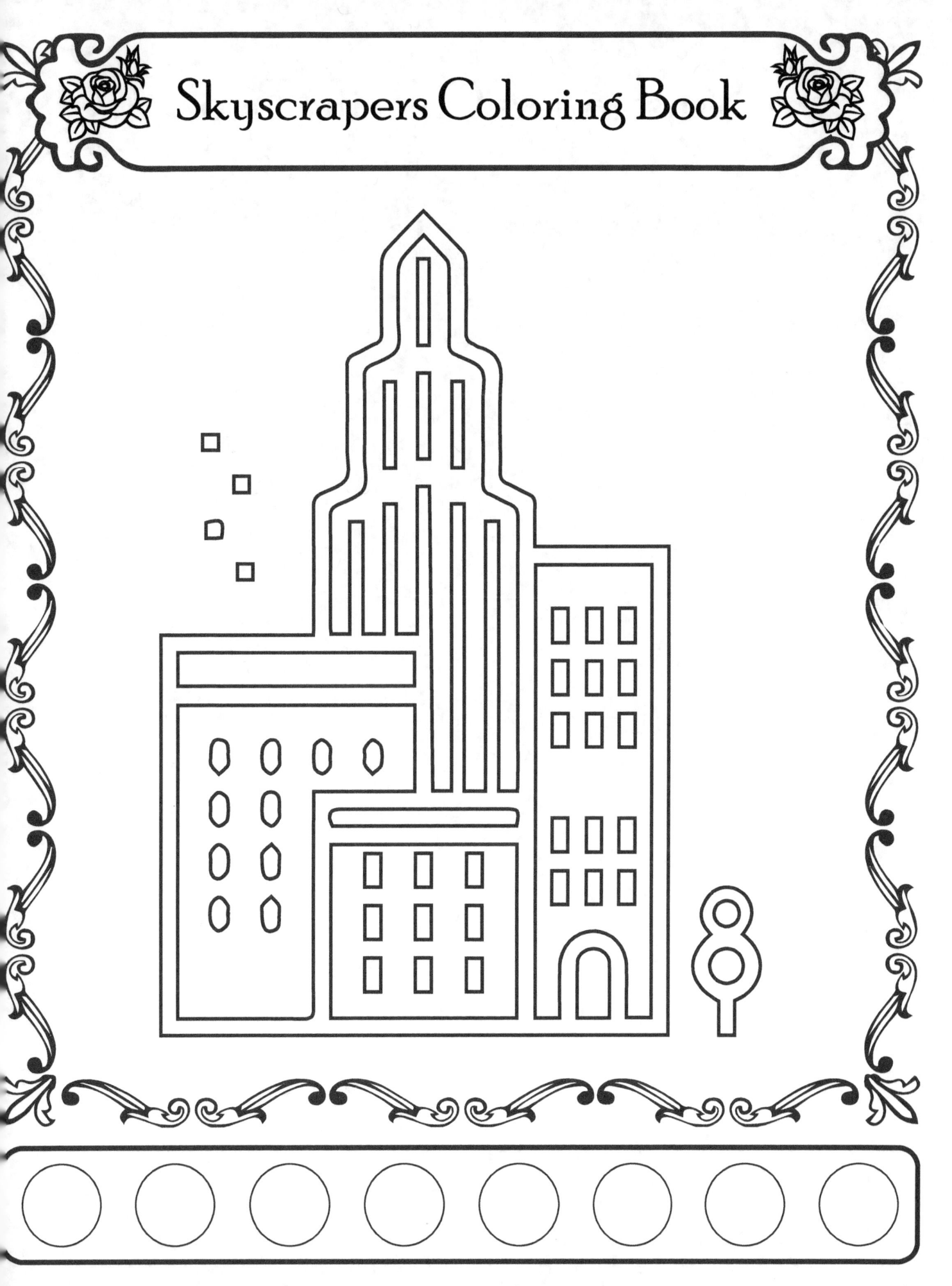

Skyscrapers Coloring Book

Skyscrapers Coloring Book

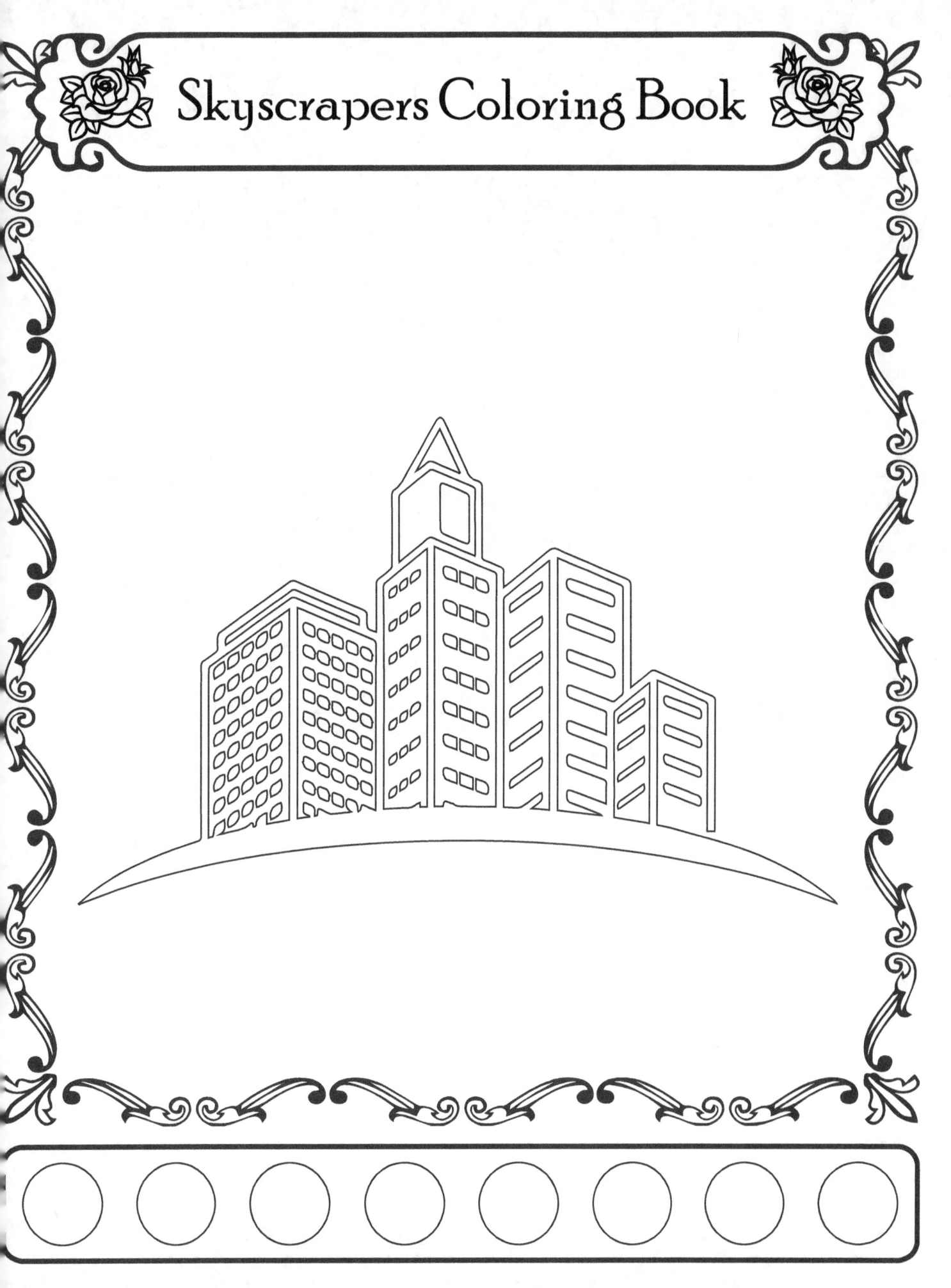

Skyscrapers Coloring Book

Skyscrapers Coloring Book

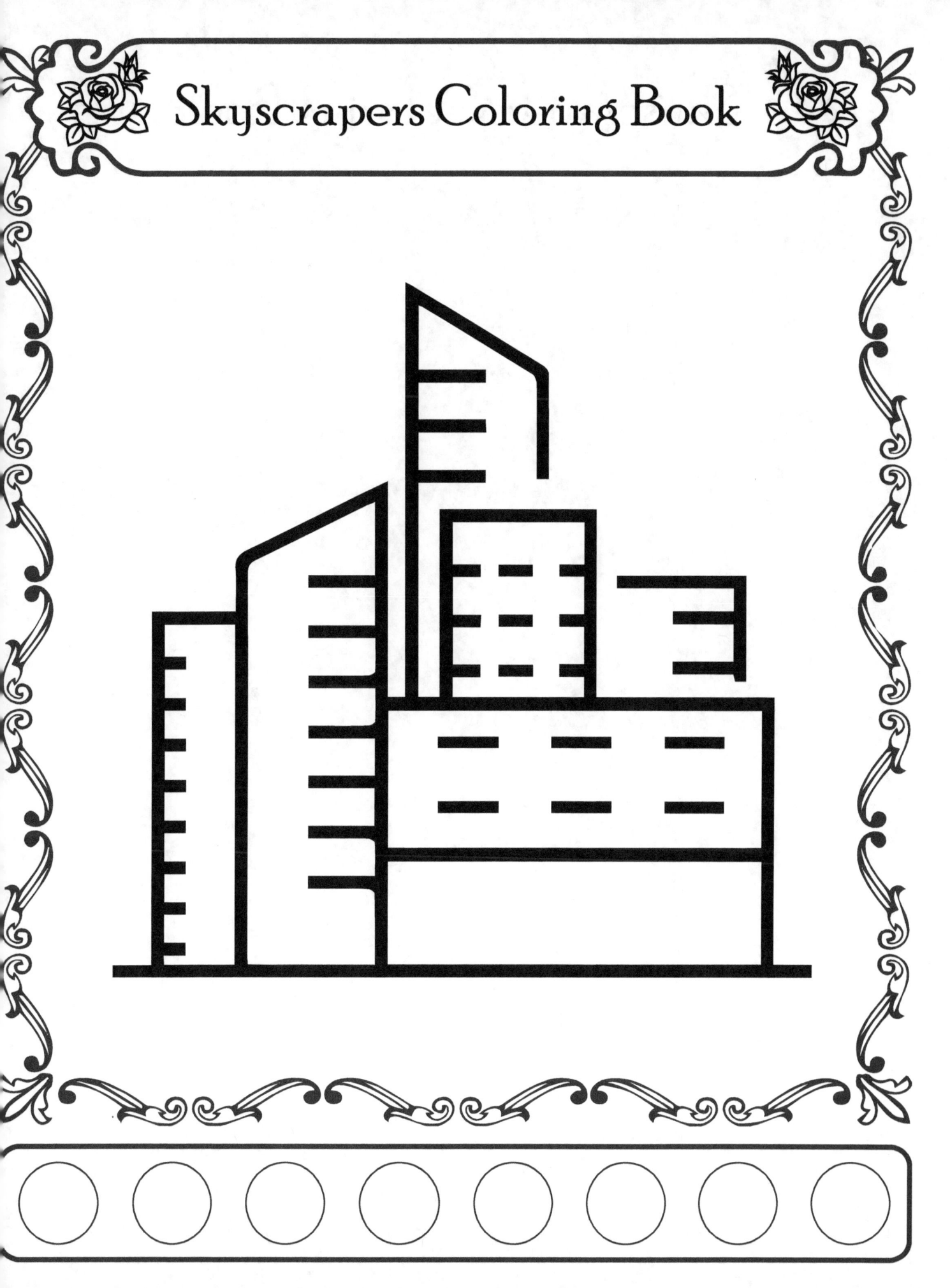

Skyscrapers Coloring Book

Skyscrapers Coloring Book

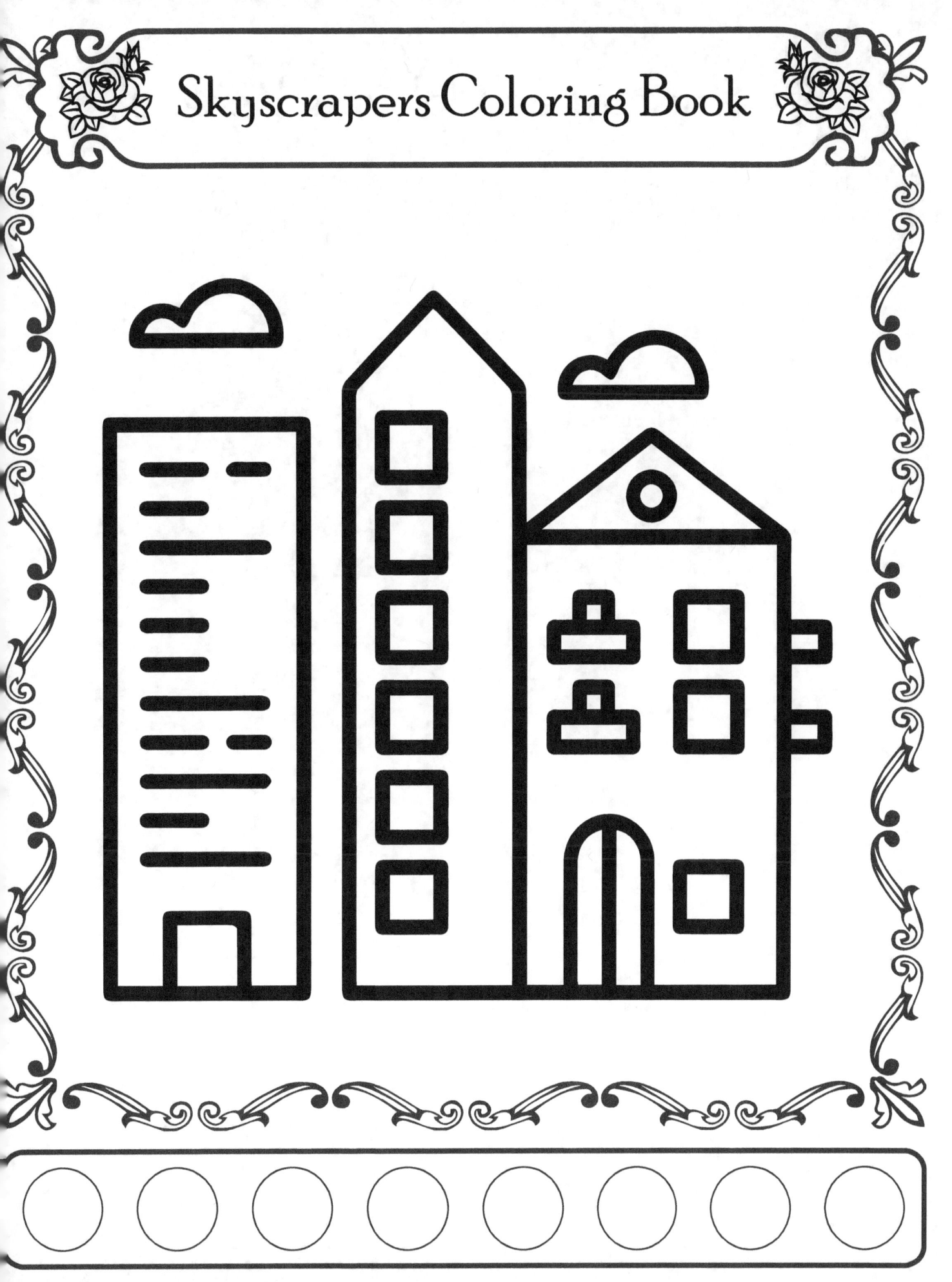

Skyscrapers Coloring Book

Skyscrapers Coloring Book

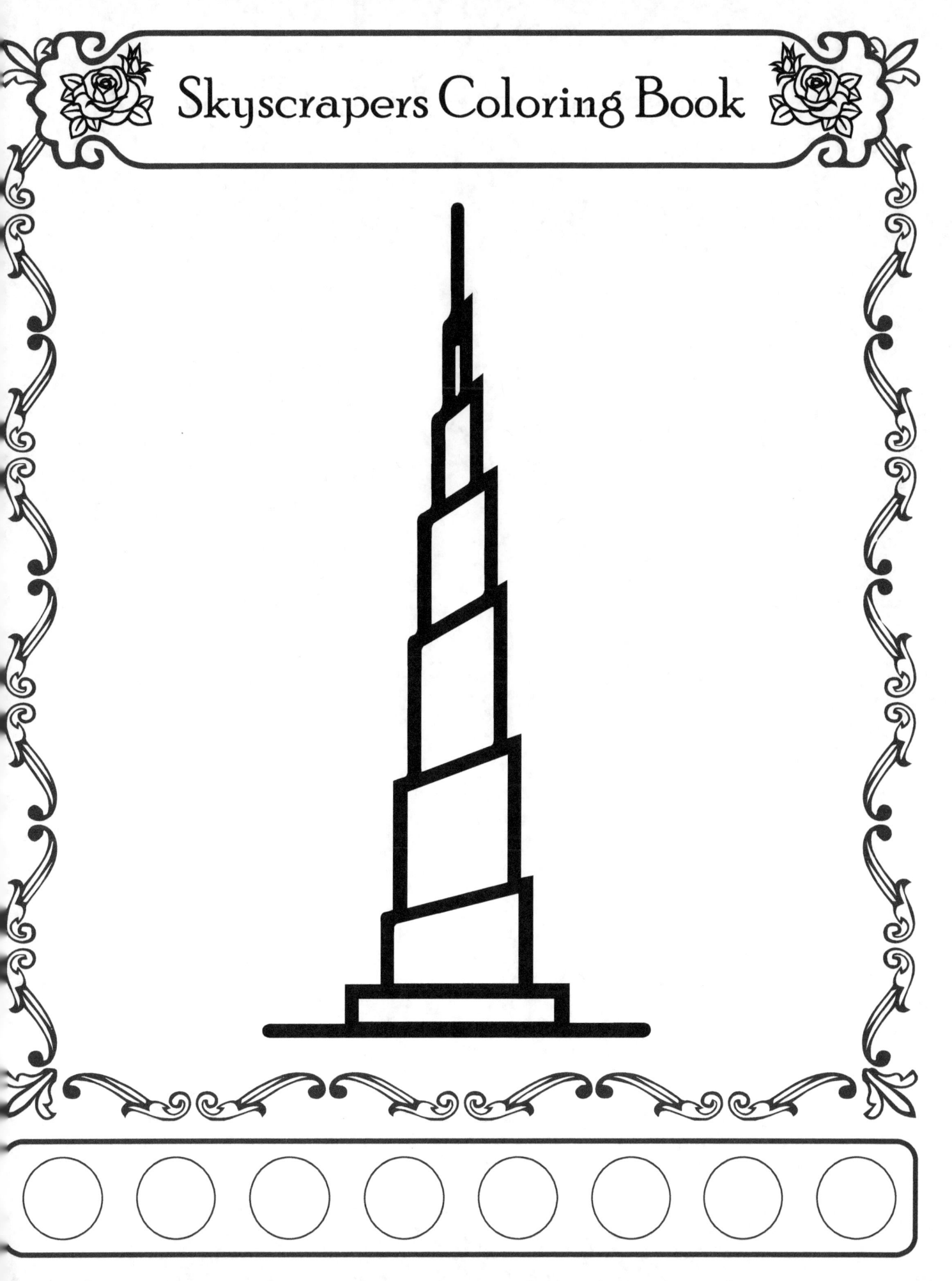

Skyscrapers Coloring Book

Skyscrapers Coloring Book

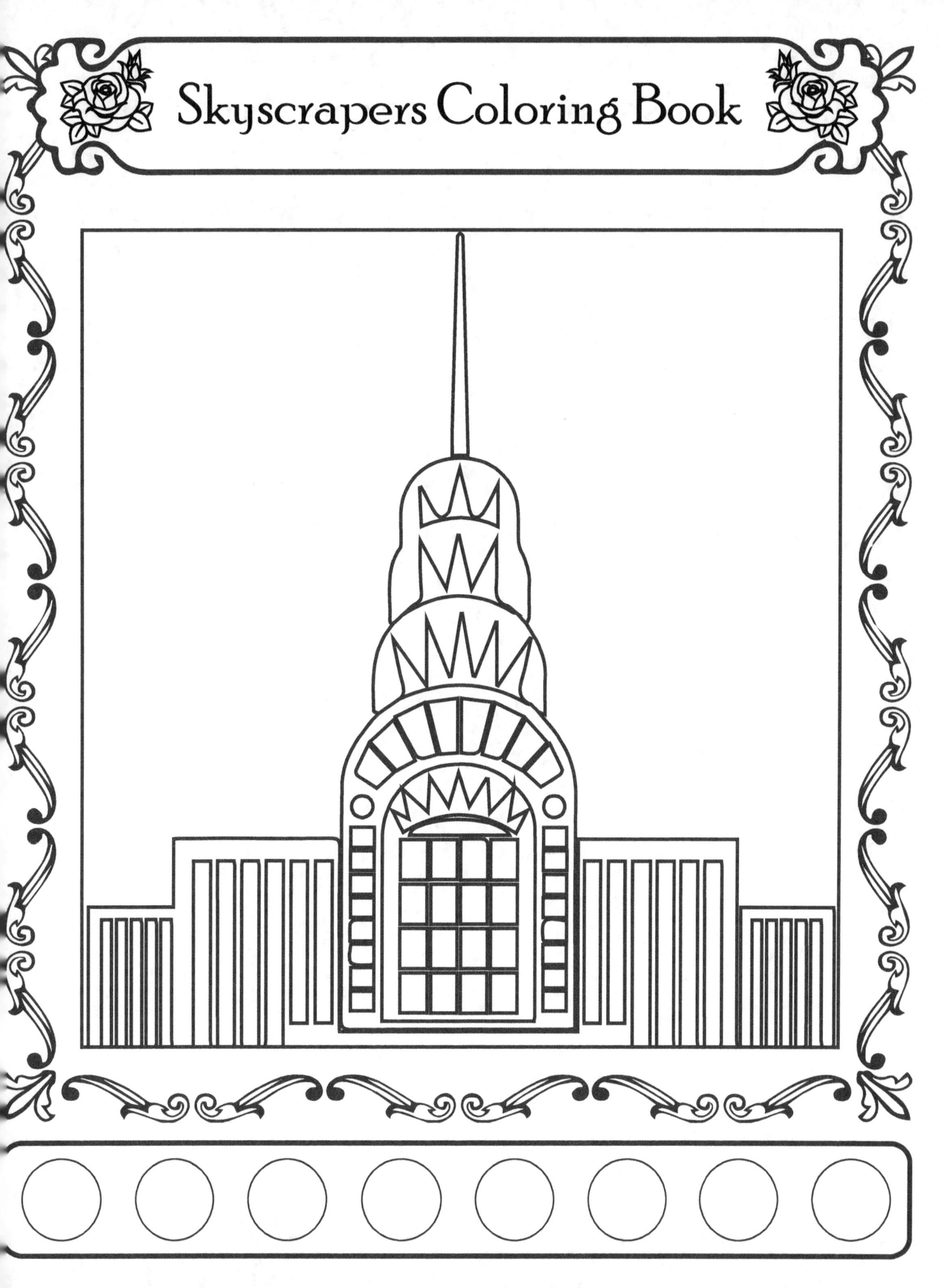

Skyscrapers Coloring Book

Skyscrapers Coloring Book

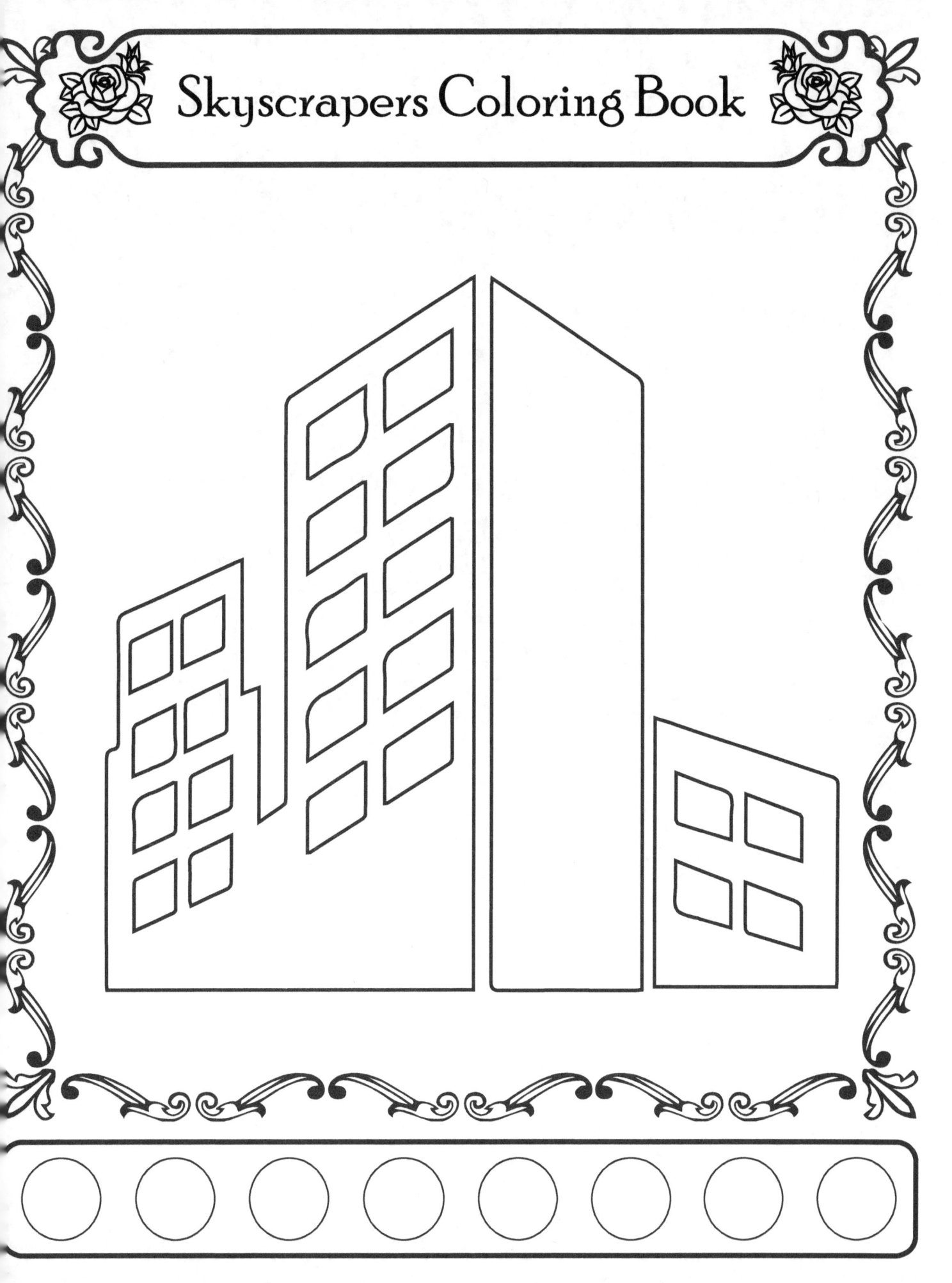

Skyscrapers Coloring Book

Skyscrapers Coloring Book

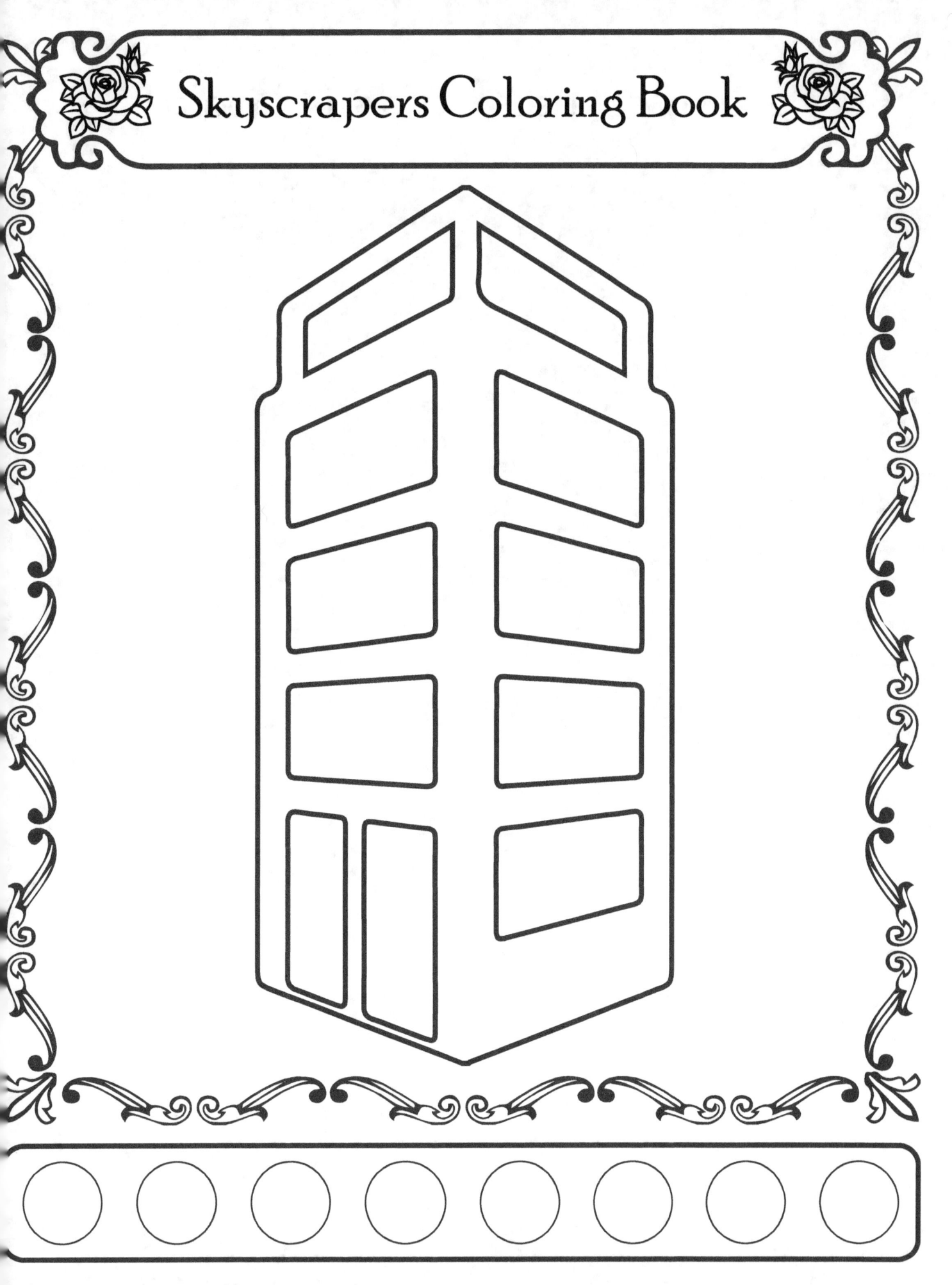

Skyscrapers Coloring Book

Skyscrapers Coloring Book

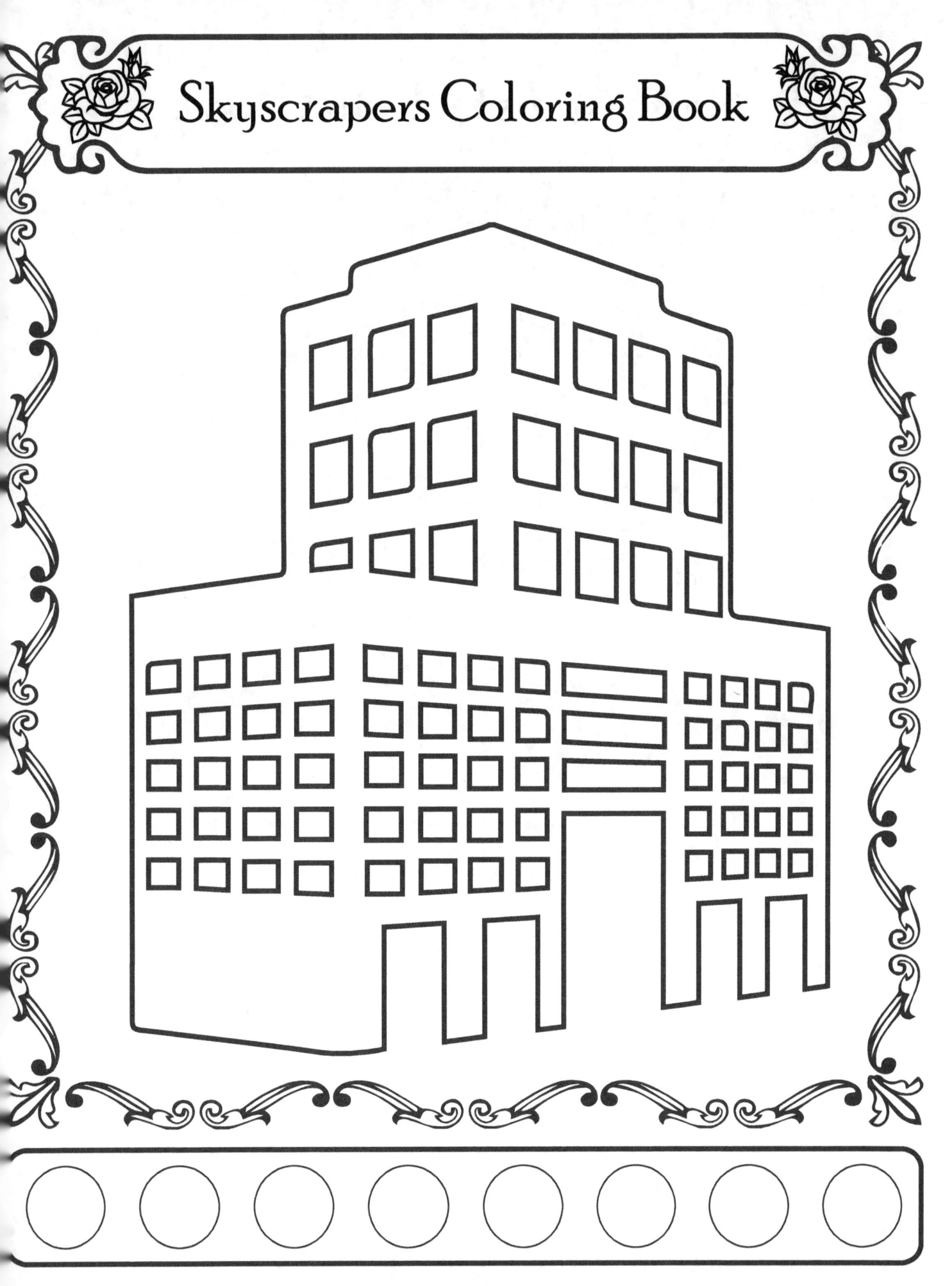

Skyscrapers Coloring Book

Skyscrapers Coloring Book

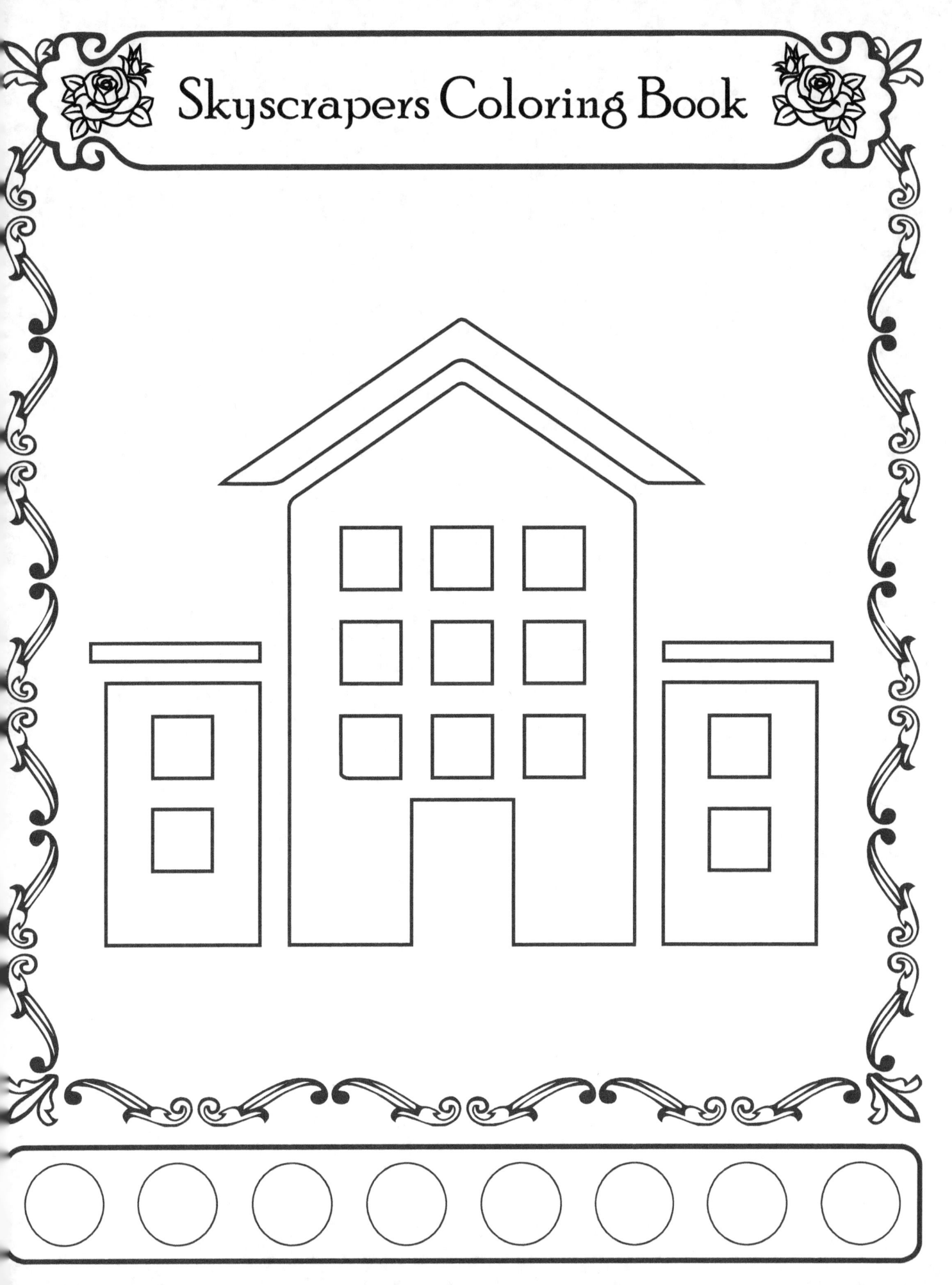

Skyscrapers Coloring Book

Skyscrapers Coloring Book

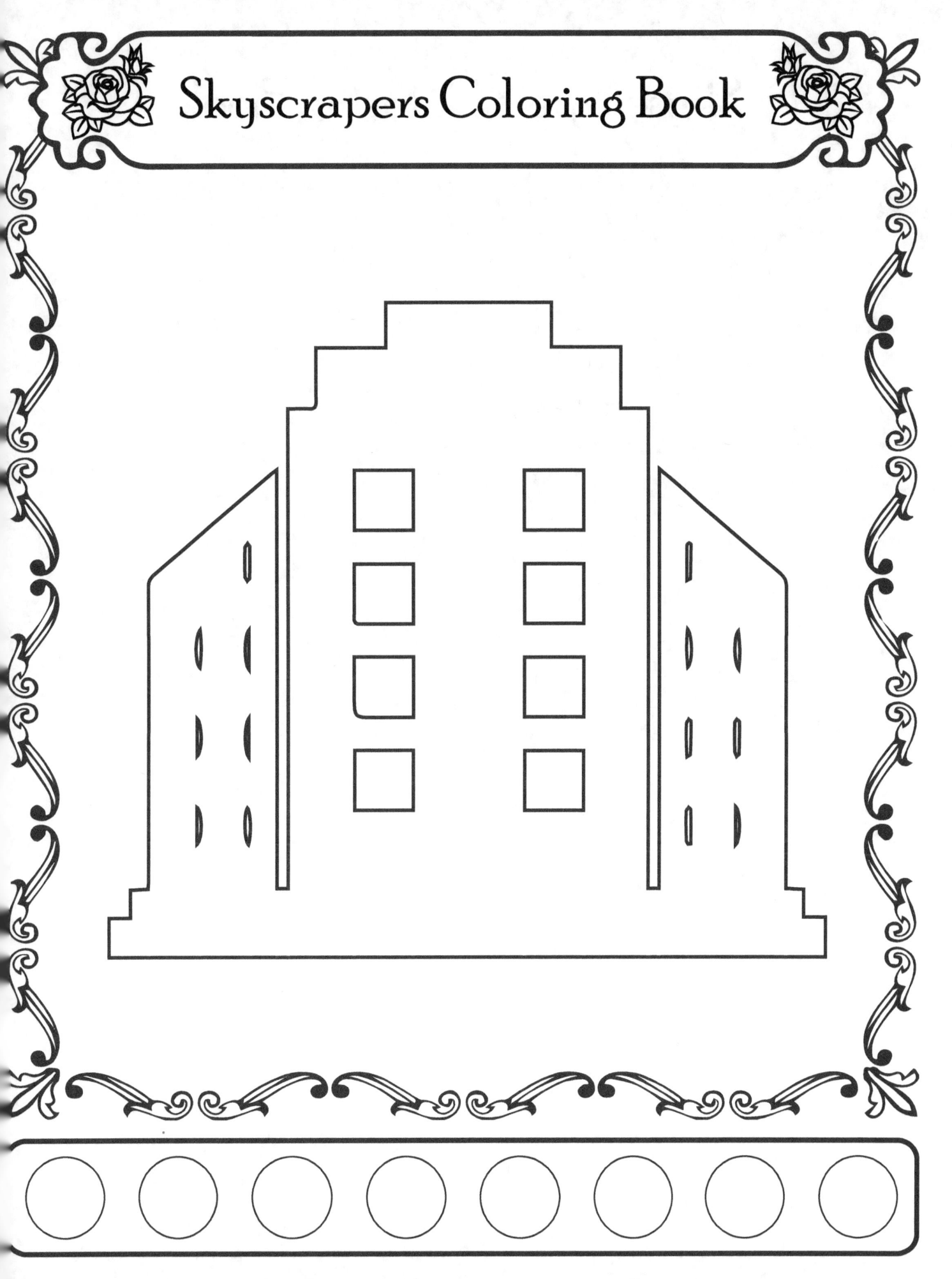

Skyscrapers Coloring Book

Skyscrapers Coloring Book

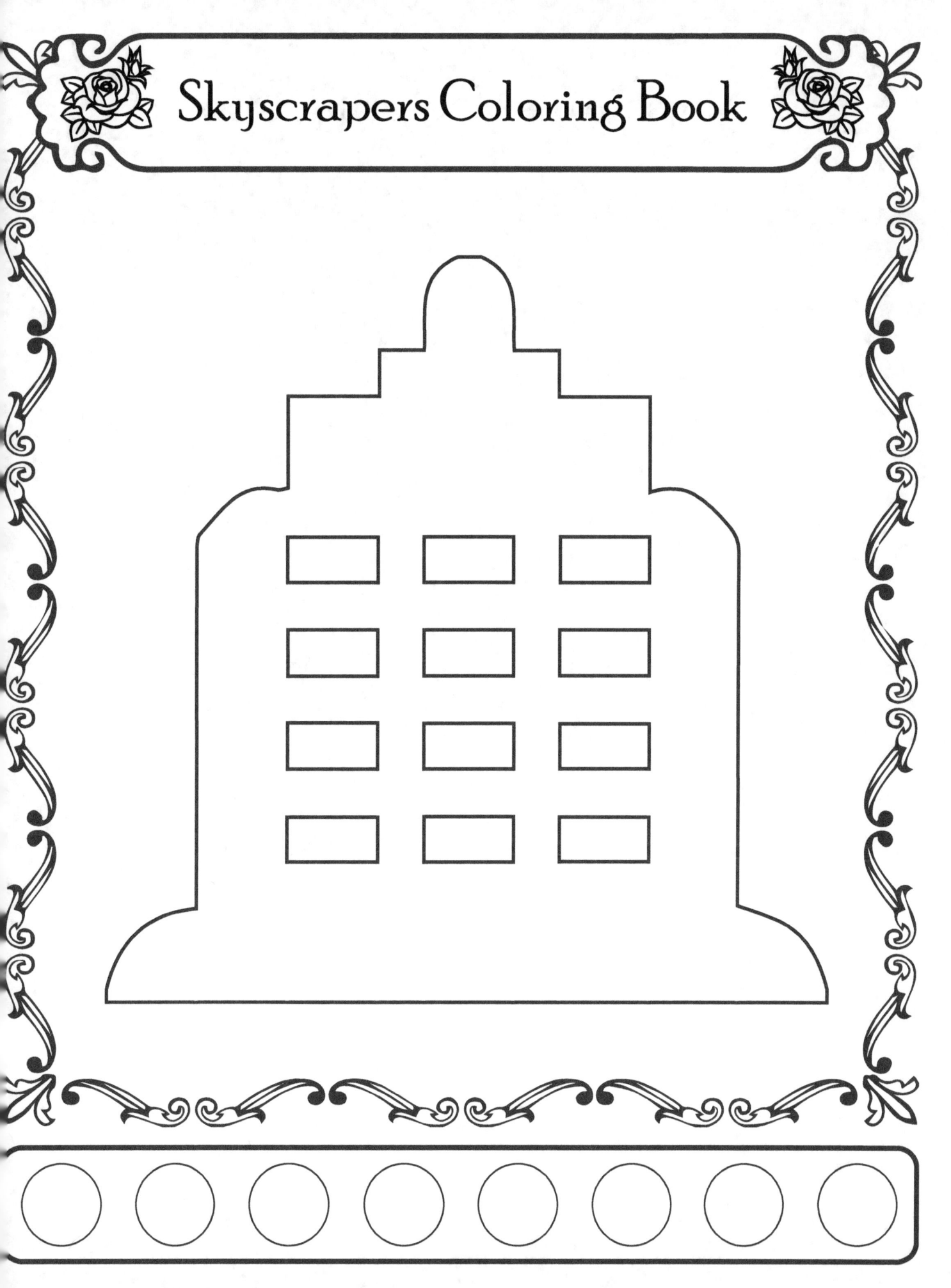

Skyscrapers Coloring Book

Skyscrapers Coloring Book

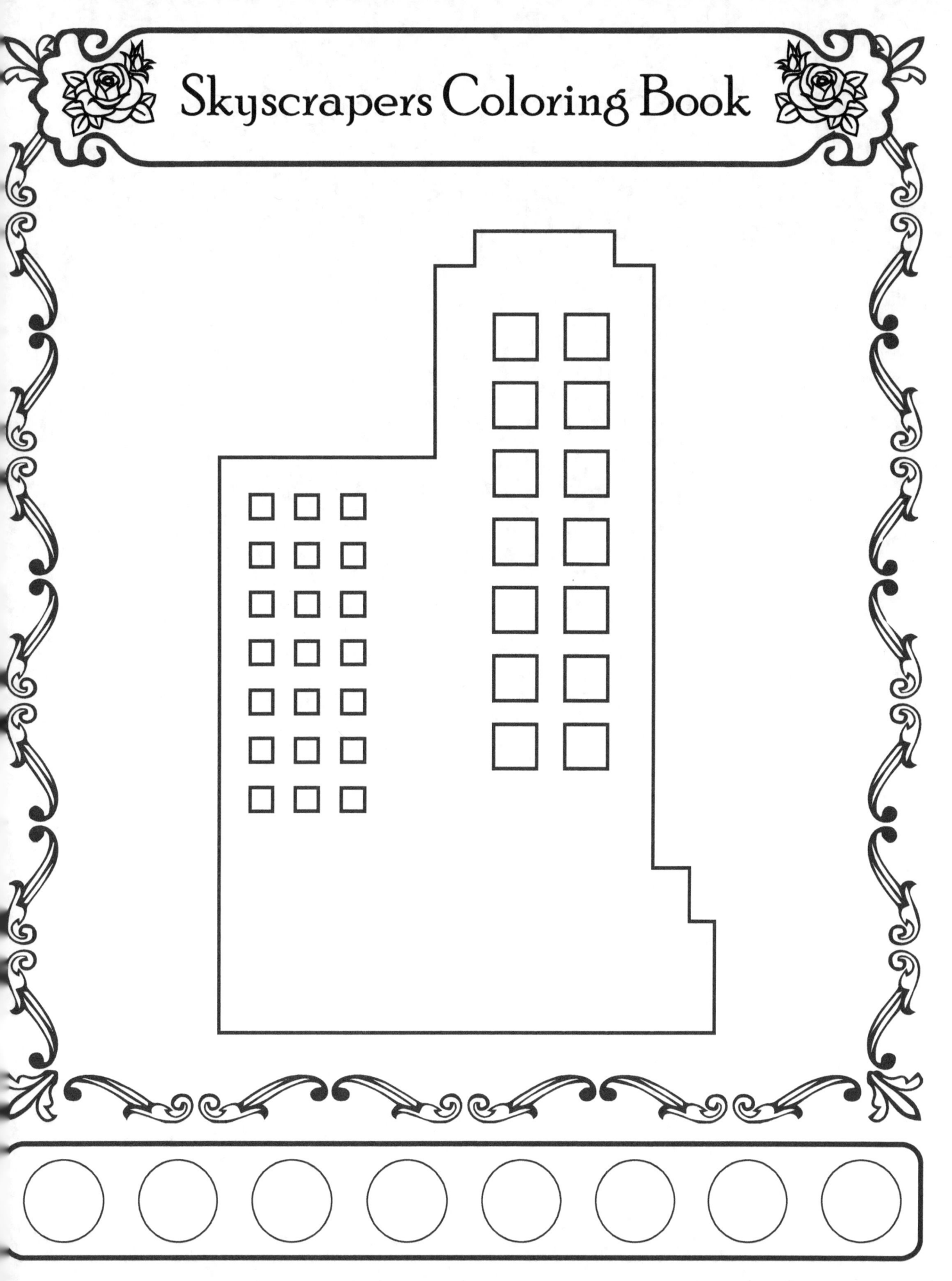

Skyscrapers Coloring Book

Skyscrapers Coloring Book

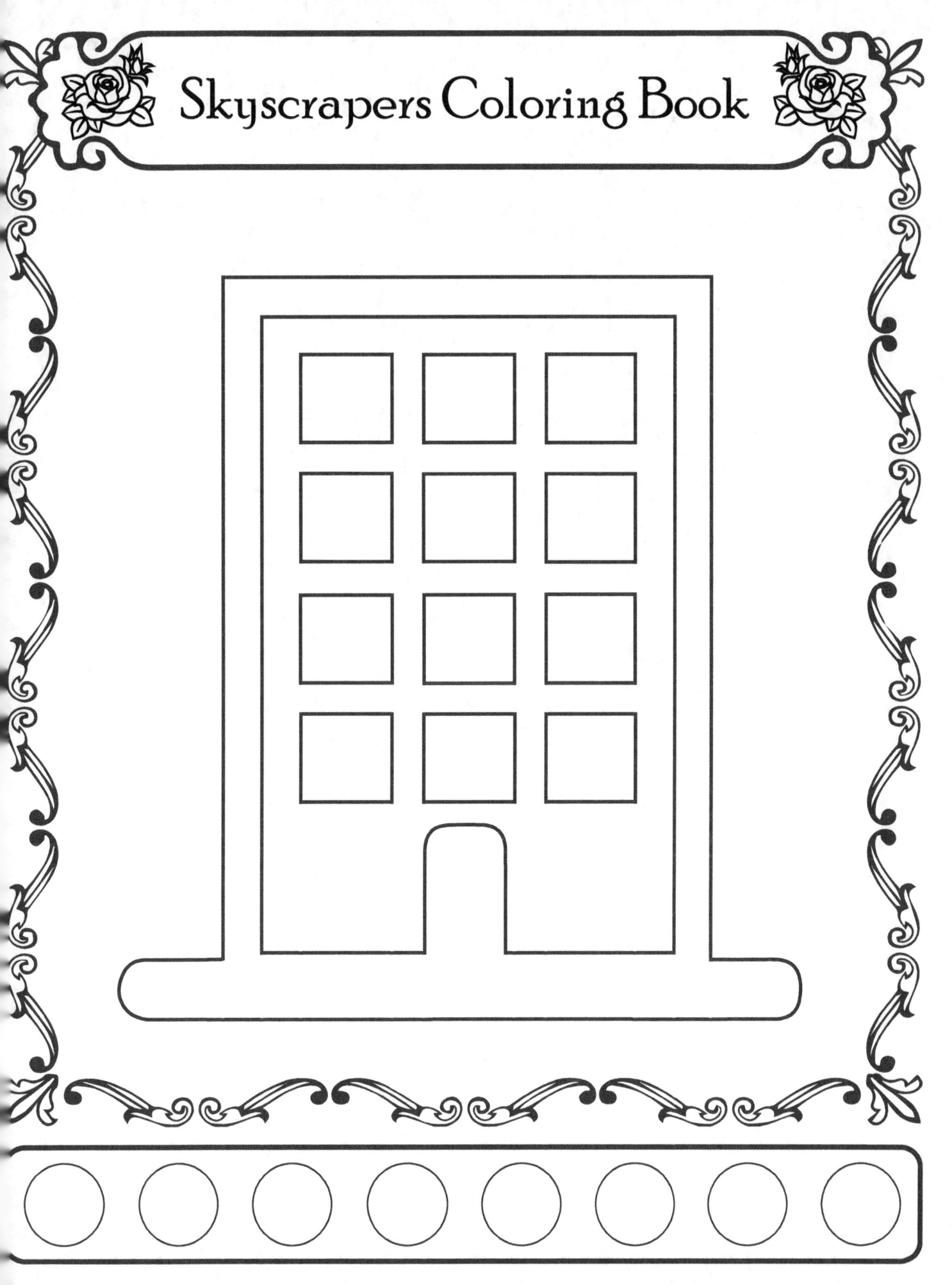

Skyscrapers Coloring Book